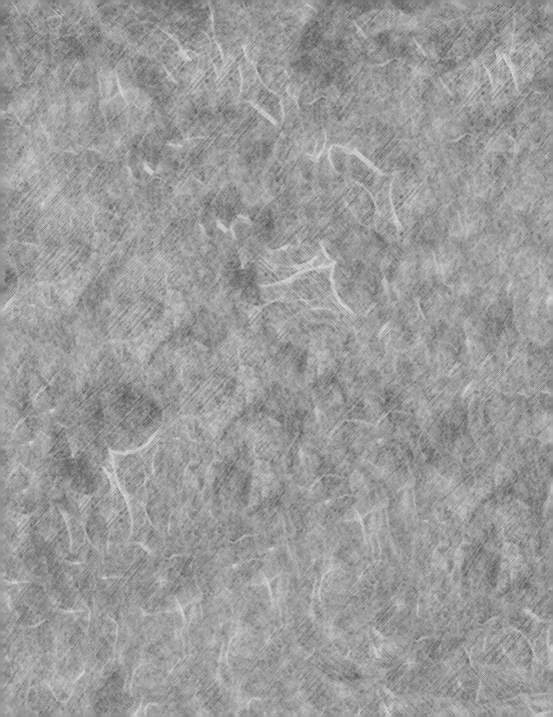

Presented to

_____

by

_____

on

_____

the
Jesus
Storybook

Every story whispers his name

Bible

DEDICATION

For Harry, Olivia, Emily, Eleanor and Jonathan
Because the Fairy Tale really does come true!
SLJ

For Alex, my lovely wife, without whose help I could
never have completed such an enormous book.
Jago

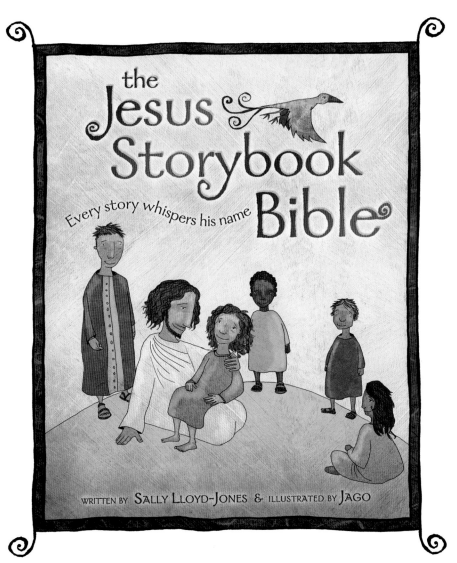

the Jesus Storybook Bible

Every story whispers his name

WRITTEN BY SALLY LLOYD-JONES & ILLUSTRATED BY JAGO

ZONDERVAN.com/
AUTHORTRACKER
follow your favorite authors

ZONDERkidz™
.com

ZONDERKIDZ

The Jesus Storybook Bible
Copyright © 2007 by Zondervan
Text copyright © 2007 by Sally Lloyd-Jones
Illustration copyright © 2007 by Jago Silver

Requests for information should be addressed to:

Zondervan, *Grand Rapids, Michigan 49530*

Library of Congress Cataloging-in-Publication Data

Lloyd-Jones, Sally.
    The Jesus Storybook Bible : every story whispers his name / by
  Sally Lloyd-Jones ; illustrated by Jago.
      p. cm.
    ISBN 978-0-310-71878-9 (printed hardcover)
     1. Bible stories, English. I. Jago, ill. II. Title.
  BS551.3.J66 2007
  220'.505–dc22
                                                  2006025327

Published in association with the literary agency of Ann Spangler & Company, 1420 Pontiac Road Southeast, Grand Rapids, Michigan 49506.

Zonderkidz is a trademark of Zondervan.

Editor: Catherine DeVries
Art Direction: Kristine Nelson
Interior Design: Julie Chen
Production Assistance: Sherri Hoffman and P.J. Lyons
Agency: Linda Kenney, Ann Spangler and Company
Theological Review: Kathy Keller, M.A. Theological Studies, Gordon - Conwell Seminary

Printed in China

11 12 13 14 /SCC/ 20 19 18 17 16

Acknowledgements

" 'Tis not that I did choose Thee,
For Lord, that could not be;
This heart would still refuse Thee,
Hadst Thou not chosen me ...

My heart owns none before Thee,
For Thy rich grace I thirst;
This knowing, if I love Thee,
Thou must have loved me first."

Josiah Conder, 1836

I owe an enormous debt of gratitude to those without whom I could not have done this book. To Dr. Timothy Keller, whose teaching informs every story and from whom I have liberally borrowed: for his wisdom; for giving me a vocabulary of faith; for opening my eyes to the wonder of Grace. To my parents who first told me The Story, as a four year old — and to Hanmer who embodied it. To all my friends at Zondervan — the amazing Kris, and especially to my editor, Catherine, who caught the vision and kept it alive. To our dedicated outside team — Julie and Linda. To the utterly brilliant Jago — what a privilege to work with you. (I'm your biggest fan.) To the Keiths, the Brownes, Paul for always giving me a warm place to write. To Todd and Laura and my endlessly patient family and friends — you know who you are! — who talked me off ledges and prayed for me. And, of course, everything to the One who is my Life — all the praise goes to Him.   —SLJ

TABLE OF CONTENTS

From the Old Testament

From the New Testament

Quotations

"Jesus said, 'I am the Beginning and the Ending.'"

Revelation 22:13 (paraphrase)

"Beginning with Moses and all the Prophets,
Jesus explained to them what was said in all the Scriptures
concerning himself."

Luke 24:27 (NIV)

"Jesus said, 'God loved the people of the world so much
that he gave his only Son.
So that anyone who believes in him
will have eternal life and never really die.
He did not send his Son into the world to punish people.
He sent him to rescue them.'"

John 3:16 – 17 (paraphrase)

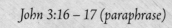

"Jesus said, 'I am the light that has come into the world.
No one who believes in me will stay
in the dark hiding anymore.' "

John 12:46 (paraphrase)

"The Sovereign Lord will wipe away
all the tears from all the faces."

Isaiah 25:8

"I had always felt life first as a story:
and if there is a story there is a story-teller."
G K Chesterton

The Story and The Song

Introduction from Psalm 19 and Hebrews 1

The Heavens are singing
about how great God is;
and the skies are shouting it out,
"See what God has made!"
Day after day... Night after night...
They are speaking to us.

Psalm 19:1-2 (paraphrase)

God wrote, "I love you" — he wrote it in the sky, and on the earth, and under the sea. He wrote his message everywhere! Because God created everything in his world to reflect him like a mirror — to show us what he is like, to help us know him, to make our hearts sing.

The way a kitten chases her tail. The way red poppies grow wild. The way a dolphin swims.

And God put it into words, too, and wrote it in a book called "the Bible."

NOAH   MOSES   DAVID   LEAH   DANIEL

Now, some people think the Bible is a book of rules, telling you what you should and shouldn't do. The Bible certainly does have some rules in it. They show you how life works best. But the Bible isn't mainly about you and what you should be doing. It's about God and what he has done.

MARY PETER JOSEPH ABRAHAM SAUL

Other people think the Bible is a book of heroes, showing you people you should copy. The Bible does have some
heroes in it, but (as you'll soon find out) most of the people
in the Bible aren't heroes at all. They make some big mis-
takes (sometimes on purpose). They get afraid and run
away. At times they are downright mean.

No, the Bible isn't a book of rules, or a book of heroes. The Bible is most of all a Story. It's an adventure story about a young Hero who comes from a far country to win back his lost treasure. It's a love story about a brave Prince who leaves his palace, his throne — everything — to rescue the one he loves. It's like the most wonderful of fairy tales that has come true in real life!

You see, the best thing about this Story is — it's true.

There are lots of stories in the Bible, but all the stories are telling one Big Story. The Story of how God loves his children and comes to rescue them.

It takes the whole Bible to tell this Story. And at the center of the Story, there is a baby. Every Story in the Bible whispers his name. He is like the missing piece in a puzzle — the piece that makes all the other pieces fit together, and suddenly you can see a beautiful picture.

And this is no ordinary baby. This is the Child upon whom everything would depend. This is the Child who would one day — but wait. Our Story starts where all good stories start. Right at the very beginning ...

The beginning: a perfect home

The Song of Creation, from Genesis 1 – 2

IN THE BEGINNING, there was nothing.

Nothing to hear. Nothing to feel. Nothing to see.

Only emptiness. And darkness. And ... nothing but nothing.

But God was there. And God had a wonderful Plan.

"I'll take this emptiness," God said, "and I'll fill it up! Out of the darkness, I'm going to make light! And out of the nothing, I'm going to make ... EVERYTHING!"

Like a mommy bird flutters her wings over her eggs to help her babies hatch, God hovered over the deep, silent darkness. He was making life happen.

God spoke. That's all. And whatever he said, it happened.

God said, "Hello light!" and light
shone into the darkness. God called the
light, "Day" and the darkness, "Night."
"You're good," God said. And they were.

Then God said, "Hello sea! Hello sky!" and a great
space opened up, wide and deep and high. "You're
good," God said. And they were.

Then God said, "Hello land!" and there — splashing
up through the oceans — came cliffs, mountains, sandy
beaches. "You're good," God said. And they were.

"Hello trees!" God said. "Hello grass and flowers!"
And everything everywhere burst into life. He made
buds bud; shoots shoot; flowers flower. "You're good,"
God said. And they were.

"Hello stars!" God said. "Hello sun! Hello moon!"
And whizzing into the darkness came fiery globes,
spinning around and around — whirling orange and
purple and golden planets. "You're good," God said.
And they were.

"Hello birds!" God said. And with a fluttering and flapping and chirping and singing, birds filled the skies. "Hello fish!" God said. And with a darting and dashing and wriggling and splashing, fish filled the seas! "You're good," God said. And they were.

Then God said, "Hello animals!" And everyone came out to play. The earth was filled with noisy noises — growling and gobbling and snapping and snorting and happy skerfuffling. "You're good," God said. And they were.

God saw all that he had made and he loved them.
And they were lovely because he loved them.

But God saved the best for last. From the beginning,
God had a shining dream in his heart. He would make
people to share his Forever Happiness. They would be
his children, and the world would be their perfect home.

So God breathed life into Adam and Eve. When they opened their eyes, the first thing they ever saw was God's face.

And when God saw them he was like a new dad. "You look like me," he said. "You're the most beautiful thing I've ever made!"

God loved them with all of his heart. And they were lovely because he loved them.

And Adam and Eve joined in the song of the stars and the streams and the wind in the trees, the wonderful song of love to the one who made them. Their hearts were filled with happiness. And nothing ever made them sad or lonely or sick or afraid.

God looked at everything he had made. "Perfect!"
he said. And it was.

But all the stars and the mountains and oceans and
galaxies and everything were nothing compared to how
much God loved his children. He would move heaven
and earth to be near them. Always. Whatever happened,
whatever it cost him, he would always love them.

And so it was that the wonderful
love story began…

The terrible lie

Adam and Eve lose everything, from Genesis 3

ADAM AND EVE lived happily together in their beautiful new home. And everything was perfect — for a while.

Until the day when everything went wrong.

God had a horrible enemy. His name was Satan. Satan had once been the most beautiful angel, but he didn't want to be just an angel — he wanted to be God. He grew proud and evil and full of hate, and God had to send him out of heaven. Satan was seething with anger and looking for a way to hurt God. He wanted to stop God's plan, stop this love story, right there. So he disguised himself as a snake and waited in the garden.

Now, God had given Adam and Eve only one rule: "Don't eat the fruit on that tree," God told them. "Because if you do, you'll think you know everything. You'll stop trusting me. And then death and sadness and tears will come."

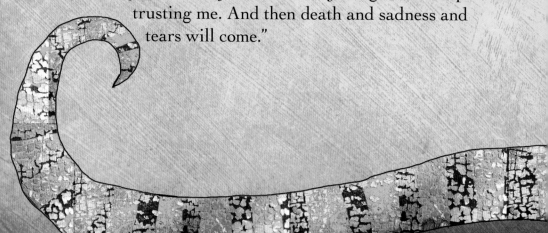

(You see, God knew if they ate the fruit, they would think they didn't need him. And they would try to make themselves happy without him. But God knew there was no such thing as happiness without him, and life without him wouldn't be life at all.)

As soon as the snake saw his chance, he slithered silently up to Eve. "Does God really love you?" the serpent whispered. "If he does, why won't he let you eat the nice, juicy, delicious fruit? Poor you, perhaps God doesn't want you to be happy."

The snake's words hissed into her ears and sunk down deep into her heart, like poison. *Does God love me?* Eve wondered. Suddenly she didn't know anymore.

"Just trust me," the serpent whispered. "You don't need God. One small taste, that's all, and you'll be happier than you could ever dream..."

Eve picked the fruit and ate some. And Adam ate some, too.

And a terrible lie came into the world. It would never leave. It would live on in every human heart, whispering to every one of God's children: "God doesn't love me."

And it wasn't a dream. It was a nightmare.

A dove flew from Adam's hand. A deer darted
in a thicket. It was as if they were frightened
by something. A chill was in the air. Something
strange was happening. They had always been
naked — but now they felt naked, and wrong,
and they didn't want anyone to see them. So
they hid.

Later that evening, as God was taking his walk, he
called to them. "Children?"

Usually Adam and Eve loved to hear God's
voice and would run to him. But this time, they
ran away from him and hid in the shadows.

"Where are you?" God called.

"Hiding," Adam said. "We're afraid of you."

"Did you eat the fruit I told you not to eat?" God asked them.

Adam said, "Eve made me do it!"

"What have you done?" God asked.

Eve said, "The serpent made me do it!"

And terrible pain came into God's heart. His children hadn't just broken the one rule; they had broken God's heart. They had broken their wonderful relationship with him. And now he knew everything else would break. God's creation would start to unravel, and come undone, and go wrong. From now on everything would die — even though it was all supposed to last forever.

You see, sin had come into God's perfect world. And it would never leave. God's children would be always running away from him and hiding in the dark. Their hearts would break now, and never work properly again. God couldn't let his children live forever, not in such pain, not without him. There was only one way to protect them.

"You will have to leave the garden now," God told his children, his eyes filling with tears. "This is no longer your true home, it's not the place for you anymore."

But before they left the garden, God made clothes for his children, to cover them. He gently clothed them and then he sent them away on a long, long journey — out of the garden, out of their home.

Well, in another story, it would all be over and that would have been...

The End.

But not in this Story.

God loved his children too much to let the story end there. Even though he knew he would suffer, God had a plan — a magnificent dream. One day, he would get his children back. One day, he would make the world their perfect home again. And one day, he would wipe away every tear from their eyes.

You see, no matter what, in spite of everything, God would love his children — with a Never Stopping, Never Giving Up, Unbreaking, Always and Forever Love.

And though they would forget him, and run from him, deep in their hearts, God's children would miss him always, and long for him — lost children yearning for their home.

Before they left the garden, God whispered a promise to Adam and Eve: "It will not always be so! I will come to rescue you! And when I do, I'm going to do battle against the snake. I'll get rid of the sin and the dark and the sadness you let in here. I'm coming back for you!"

And he would. One day, God himself would come.

A new beginning

Noah's ark, from Genesis 6 – 9

NOAH

TIME PASSED and many people filled the earth. Everyone everywhere had forgotten about God and were only doing bad things all the time.

God's heart was filled with pain when he saw what had happened to the world he loved. Everywhere was disease and death and destruction — all the things God hates most.

Now, Noah was God's friend (which was odd in those days because no one else was). Noah listened to God. He talked to God. He just loved being with God, like you do with your best friend.

"Noah," God said. "Things have gone wrong. People have filled my world with hate instead of love. They are destroying themselves ... and each other ... and my world. I must stop them. First, we'll build an ark." (Do you know how to build an ark? Neither did Noah. Luckily, God knew and he would show him.)

"A storm is coming," God told Noah. "But I will rescue you. I promise. I'll send the animals to you — ones that creep and crawl and slither and slime and gallop and hop and bound and climb. And don't forget to pack everyone's food."

The storm was going to wash away all the hate and sadness and everything that had gone wrong, and make the world clean again. God had thought up a way to keep Noah safe, but Noah would have to trust God and do exactly what God told him.

So Noah built an ark (short for very large boat).

Noah's neighbors came out to watch … and point … and laugh, because they didn't believe Noah about the boat … or the storm … or needing to be rescued. And Noah must have looked rather silly. His boat was in the desert, the desert was nowhere near the sea, and there wasn't even a cloud in the sky. Why would anyone need an umbrella, let alone a boat?

41

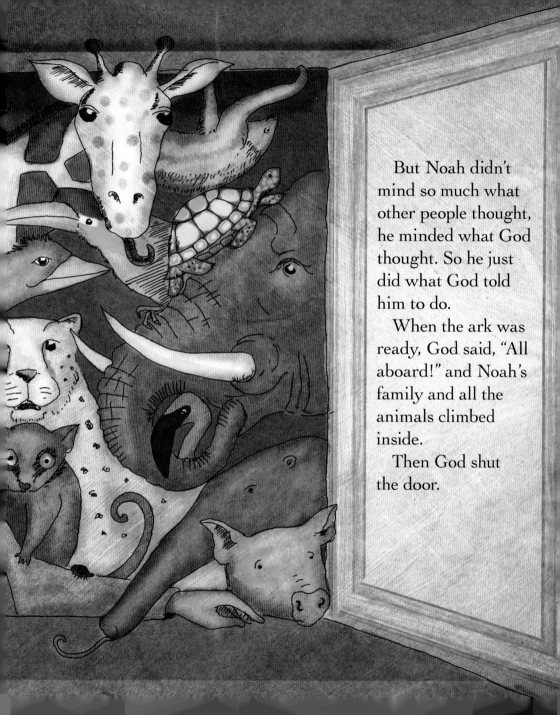

But Noah didn't mind so much what other people thought, he minded what God thought. So he just did what God told him to do.

When the ark was ready, God said, "All aboard!" and Noah's family and all the animals climbed inside.

Then God shut the door.

And it started raining — for minutes, that joined up into hours, that joined up into days, that joined up into weeks and weeks. And the rain joined up into puddles, that joined up into rivers, that joined up into lakes, that joined up into a flood that covered the whole world.

Their boat that had once seemed so big, suddenly seemed very small. But in the middle of the huge storm, in the crashing waves, in all the thunder and lightning — through it all — God was with them. And God kept them safe for 40 long days and 40 long nights.

Finally, the rain stopped. The sun came out and Noah threw open all the windows. "Hooray!" everyone shouted.

Noah sent his dove out to explore, and it wasn't long before she brought him back a fresh olive leaf. Everyone knew exactly what that meant: she had found a tree — and land! The water was going down.

At last, the boat landed quite suddenly on top of a great mountain. As soon as it was safe, God said, "Out you come!" And so they did — everyone skipping and dancing onto dry land.

The first thing Noah did was to thank God for rescuing them, just as he had promised.

And the first thing God did was make another promise. "I won't ever destroy the world again." And like a warrior who puts away his bow and arrow at the end of a great battle, God said, "See, I have hung up my bow in the clouds."

And there, in the clouds — just where the storm meets the sun — was a beautiful bow made of light.

It was a new beginning in God's world.

It wasn't long before everything went wrong again but God wasn't surprised, he knew this would happen. That's why, before the beginning of time, he had another plan — a better plan. A plan not to destroy the world, but to rescue it — a plan to one day send his own Son, the Rescuer.

God's strong anger against hate and sadness and death would come down once more — but not on his people, or his world. No, God's war bow was not pointing down at his people.

It was pointing up, into the heart of Heaven.

A giant staircase to heaven

The tower of Babel, from Genesis 11

NOAH AND HIS FAMILY lived in the land and his children had children, and those children had more children, and then those children had even more — well, you get the picture — until there were lots of people on the earth once more.

Now, back then, everyone spoke exactly the same language so you didn't need to learn Swahili or Japanese or anything because you could say, "Hello!" to anyone and they knew what you meant.

One day, everyone was talking and they came up with an idea: "Let's build ourselves a beautiful city to live in! It can be our home. And we'll be safe forever and ever." Then they had another idea: "And let's build a really tall tower to reach up to heaven!"

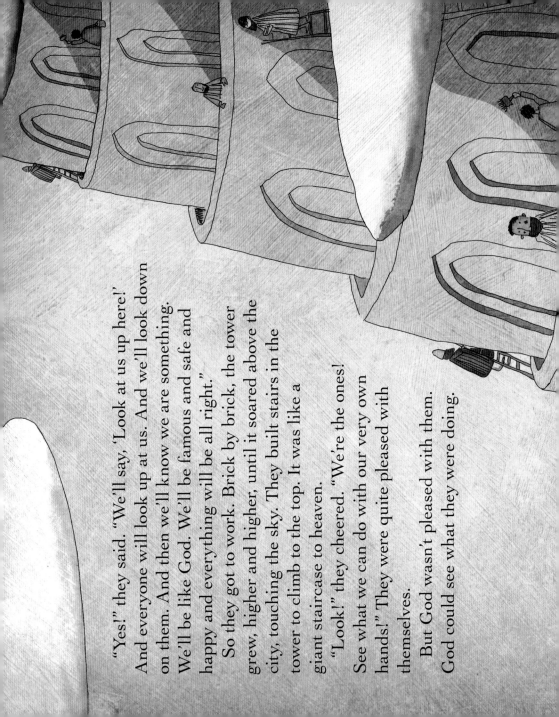

"Yes!" they said. "We'll say, 'Look at us up here!' And everyone will look up at us. And we'll look down on them. And then we'll know we are something. We'll be like God. We'll be famous and safe and happy and everything will be all right."

So they got to work. Brick by brick, the tower grew, higher and higher, until it soared above the city, touching the sky. They built stairs in the tower to climb to the top. It was like a giant staircase to heaven.

"Look!" they cheered. "We're the ones! See what we can do with our very own hands!" They were quite pleased with themselves.

But God wasn't pleased with them. God could see what they were doing.

They were trying to live without him, but God knew that wouldn't make them happy or safe or anything. If they kept on like this, they would only destroy themselves, and God loved them too much to let that happen. So he stopped their plans.

One morning, they went to work as usual but everything was different — their words were all new and funny. You see, God had given each person a completely different language! Suddenly, no one understood what anyone else was saying. Someone would say, "How do you do?" and the other person thought they said, "How ugly are you!" It wasn't funny. You could be saying something nice like, "Such a lovely morning!" and get a punch in the nose because they thought you said, "Hush up, you're boring!" (You couldn't even say, "Pardon?" to check if you'd heard right because no one understood that word either.)

It wasn't easy to work together after that, as you can only imagine. People were always quarrelling and fighting and getting in a dreadful muddle and becoming grumpier and grumpier, until at last they were all too cross to keep on building, and just had to stop.

After that, people scattered all over the world (which is how we ended up with so many different languages to this day).

You see, God knew, however high they reached, however hard they tried, people could never get back to heaven by themselves. People didn't need a staircase; they needed a Rescuer. Because the way back to heaven wasn't a staircase; it was a Person.

People could never reach up to Heaven, so Heaven would have to come down to them.

And, one day, it would.

Son of laughter

God's special promise to Abraham, from Genesis 12 – 21

YEARS PASSED and things didn't get any better. People were still just as cruel and mean to one another. They still got sick and died. God's world was still full of tears. It was never meant to be like this.

But God was getting ready to do something about it. He was going to make all the wrong things right, and he was going to do it through ... a family.

"Abraham," God said. "How many stars are there?" (God was about to tell his friend a wonderful secret.)

"Let me see," Abraham said, rolling up his sleeves. (But have you ever tried counting stars? Then you know how hard it is.) "993, 994, 997. Uh-Oh. No. Wait. 1, 2, ..." Of course, he kept losing count. "Too many!" he said.

Abraham

"Guess what!" God laughed. "I will give you so many children and grandchildren and great grandchildren, you won't be able to count them either."

Abraham couldn't help giggling at such a wonderful idea. But he stopped himself. How could he have a family? Don't be silly. He didn't have any children, let alone grandchildren.

He wiped away a tear. Anyway it was far too late for him to start having babies at his age, he was 99 years old! What could God mean?

"Abraham," God said. "Believe me."

And then God told Abraham his Secret Rescue Plan. "Abraham, I will make your family very big," God promised. "Until one day, your family will come to number more than even all the stars in the sky."

Abraham looked up at the dark night sky, thick with stars.

"You will be my special family, my people, and through you everyone on earth will be blessed!"

It was an incredible promise —
God was going to rescue the
world through Abraham's family!
One of his great-great-great grand-
children would be the Child, the
Promised One, the Rescuer.

"But it's too wonderful!" Abraham said. "How can it be true?"

"Is anything too good to be
true?" God asked. "Is anything too
wonderful for me?"

So Abraham trusted what God
said more than what his eyes could see. And he believed.

Now when Abraham's wife, Sarah, heard God's promise, she just laughed to herself. But it wasn't a happy
laugh, it had tears in it. She'd always wanted a baby,
could her dream come true? Could she really have a baby
when she was 90 years old? No, of course not, don't be
silly, it was far too late.

Sarah didn't believe God could do what he promised.
She had forgotten that when God says something, it's as
good as done. (Of course, it was as easy for God to give
her a baby son as it was for him to make all the stars in
the sky.)

Sure enough, nine months later, just as God had promised, Sarah gave birth to a baby boy. They named him Isaac, which means "son of laughter." And Sarah laughed. But this time it was a glorious, happy laugh. Her dream had come true.

God would do as he promised. He would always look after Abraham's family, his special people.

And one day, God would send another baby, a baby promised to a girl who didn't even have a husband. But this baby would bring laughter to the whole world. This baby would be everyone's dream come true.

The present

The story of Abraham and Isaac, from Genesis 22

GOD KNEW that his Secret Rescue Plan could only work if Abraham trusted him completely. God had to make sure Abraham would do whatever he asked. So, a few years later, God asked Abraham to give him a present.

Abraham liked giving presents to God. He gave God his animals. They were called "sacrifices" and they were a way to say "I love you" to God.

But this time God didn't want a lamb or a goat, God wanted Abraham to give him something more — much more. He wanted Abraham to give him his son, his only son, the son he loved — Isaac.

Put his boy on the altar and kill him as the sacrifice? How could God want him to do such a terrible thing? Abraham didn't understand. But he knew that God was his father who loved him. And so Abraham trusted him.

Early the next morning, Abraham and Isaac set off. They climbed the steep, stony trail up the mountain. Isaac carried the wood on his back. His father carried the knife and the coals.

"Papa," Isaac said, "we have everything except we forgot the lamb for the sacrifice."

"God will give us the lamb, son," Abraham said.

They built an altar and laid the wood on top. Abraham asked his son to climb on top of the wood. Isaac didn't understand but he knew his father loved him. And so he trusted him. He climbed up onto the altar and Abraham tied his boy to the wood. Isaac didn't struggle or try to run away, he just lay there quietly and didn't make a sound.

Everything was ready. Abraham took the knife. Tears were filling up his eyes. Pain was filling up his heart. His hand was shaking. He lifted the knife high into the air —

"STOP!" God said. "Don't hurt the boy. I want him to live and not die. I know now that you love me because you would have given me your only son."

Abraham felt his heart leap with joy. He unbound Isaac and folded him in his arms. Great sobs shook the old man's whole body. Scalding tears filled his eyes. And for a long time, they stayed there like that, in each other's arms, the boy and his dad.

Suddenly, Abraham saw a ram caught in some brambles — the sacrifice. God had given them what they needed just in time. The ram would die so Isaac didn't have to. And so Abraham sacrificed the ram, instead of his son.

And as they sat there on the mountaintop, watching the embers of the fire die in the cool night air, the stars above them sparkling in the velvet sky, God helped Abraham and Isaac understand something. God wanted his people to live, not die. God wanted to rescue his people, not punish them. But they must trust him.

"One day Someone will be born into your family," God promised them. "And he will bring happiness to the whole world."

God was getting ready to give the whole world a wonderful present. It would be God's way to tell his people, "I love you."

Many years later, another Son would climb another hill, carrying wood on his back. Like Isaac, he would trust his Father and do what his Father asked. He wouldn't struggle or run away.

Who was he? God's Son, his only Son — the Son he loved.

The Lamb of God.

The girl no one wanted

*The story of Jacob, Rachel, and Leah,
from Genesis 29 – 30*

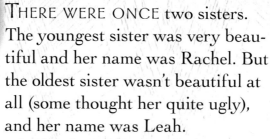

THERE WERE ONCE two sisters.
The youngest sister was very beautiful and her name was Rachel. But
the oldest sister wasn't beautiful at
all (some thought her quite ugly),
and her name was Leah.

Rachel was the kind of girl who always gets invited to
parties and chosen for the team. Everyone loved her. And
poor Leah? No one hardly even noticed her.

One day, their cousin Jacob came to stay. He was one
of Isaac's sons and he was on the run. (Jacob had stolen
and cheated and made some enemies — including his own
brother — and now he was hiding.)

The funny thing is, Jacob — of all people — was the one
God gave the special promise to, the same promise he had
given his grandfather Abraham: "I will rescue the world
through your family." (But then God chooses people we
least expect, as we'll see.)

Jacob stayed a long time working for his Uncle Laban.

One day, Laban said, "Jacob, I've decided to pay you for
your work. What do you want?" A sudden thought struck
him. "How about one of my daughters?"

Jacob looked at Rachel and he looked at Leah. Who would he choose? Of course, he chose Rachel.

"I'll work seven years for free!" Jacob said. "If I can marry Rachel."

So Jacob worked seven years and, at last, his wedding day arrived.

But that night, Laban played a nasty trick on Jacob. Instead of sending Rachel to marry Jacob, he sent Leah. (Now, in those days, they didn't have electricity, so it was dark in their tent and, besides, women wore veils and you couldn't see their faces properly. So Jacob suspected nothing.)

The next morning, Jacob woke up — and screamed. His new wife was lying beside him but it wasn't Rachel — it was Leah. Jacob jumped out of bed. "Laban!" he cried. "You scoundrel!"

But Laban said, "Work for me another seven years and then you can marry Rachel."

So Jacob worked for Laban another seven years and, at last, Rachel became his wife. Now Jacob had two wives, but of his two wives, Jacob loved Rachel the best.

"No one loves me," Leah said. "I'm too ugly."

But God didn't think she was ugly. And when he saw that Leah was not loved and that no one wanted her, God chose her — to love her specially, to give her a very important job. One day, God was going to rescue the whole world — through Leah's family.

Now when Leah knew that God loved her, in her heart, suddenly it didn't matter anymore whether her husband loved her the best, or if she was the prettiest. Someone had chosen her, someone did love her — with a Never Stopping, Never Giving Up, Unbreaking, Always and Forever Love.

So when Leah had a baby boy she called him Judah, which means, "This time I will praise the Lord!" And that's just what she did.

And you'll never guess what job God gave Leah. You see, when God looked at Leah, he saw a princess. And sure enough, that's exactly what she became. One of Leah's children's children's children would be a prince — the Prince of Heaven — God's Son.

This Prince would love God's people. They wouldn't need to be beautiful for him to love them. He would love them with all of his heart. And they would be beautiful because he loved them.

Like Leah.

75

The forgiving prince

Joseph and his brothers, from Genesis 37 – 46

JACOB HAD TWELVE SONS but of all his sons, Joseph was his favorite.

One day, Jacob gave Joseph a splendid new robe. It was beautiful and rich with all the colors of the rainbow, but it made Joseph's brothers jealous — they wanted rich rainbow robes, too.

Then to make matters worse, Joseph kept on having these special dreams: "I dreamed I was the greatest! I was king!" Joseph told his brothers. "And you all bowed down to me!"

Now I'm sure you know, even if Joseph didn't, that telling your brothers things like that isn't a very good idea. Joseph's brothers hated him even more. They wanted to kill Joseph and his dreams.

And one day that's exactly what they tried to do.

They tore Joseph's rainbow robe off him and sold him to slave traders — for 20 pieces of silver.

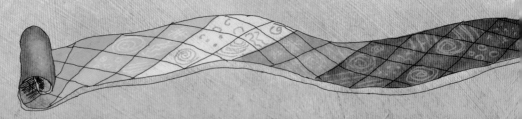

The traders took Joseph to Egypt and made him into a slave. The brothers went home and lied to their father, telling him that Joseph was dead.

That's the end of that dreamer! they thought. But they were wrong. God had a magnificent dream for Joseph's life and even when it looked like everything had gone wrong, God would use it all to help make the dream come true. God

would use everything that was happening to Joseph to do something good.

Meanwhile though, things were not looking good for Joseph in Egypt. He was far from home and from his dad. Then he got blamed for something he didn't do, and, even though he had done nothing wrong, he was punished and thrown in jail. But God had not left Joseph.

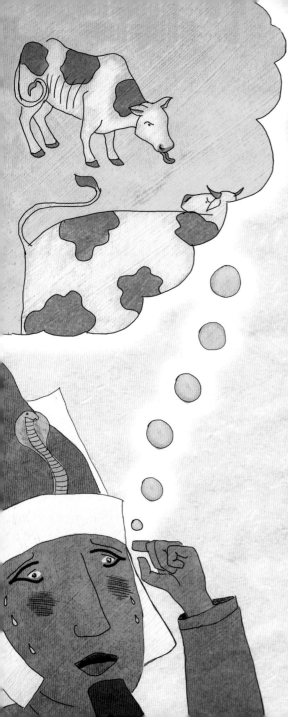

One night, Pharaoh (king of Egypt) had a scary dream about thin cows gobbling up fat cows. What on earth did it mean? He didn't know. But Joseph was a dream expert so Pharaoh sent for him. "It means a famine is coming," Joseph explained. "There won't be enough food."

Pharaoh was so pleased by Joseph's skill that he immediately took Joseph out of jail and made him a prince.

Now back home, Joseph's brothers had run out of food and everyone was hungry. God's special family was in danger — if they didn't get food soon they would starve to death. So Joseph's brothers traveled to Egypt to buy food.

They came and knelt before the new prince. His brothers didn't know that the prince was Joseph. But Joseph knew who they were. Joseph's dream, the one about his brothers bowing down to him, was coming true.

"It's me!" Joseph cried.

When they saw it was Joseph, his brothers were afraid. They had wronged Joseph. They had sinned and they knew it. Now Joseph would certainly punish them.

But Joseph looked at his brothers and his eyes filled with tears. Even though his brothers had hurt him and hated him and wanted him dead — in spite of everything — he couldn't stop loving them.

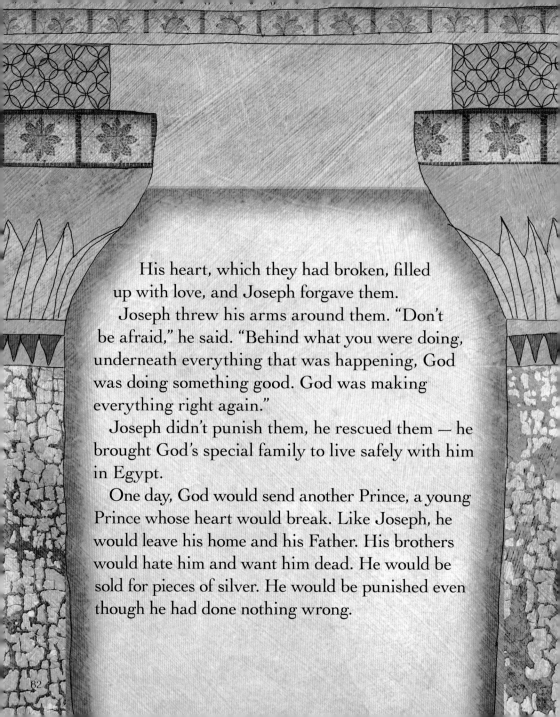

His heart, which they had broken, filled up with love, and Joseph forgave them.

Joseph threw his arms around them. "Don't be afraid," he said. "Behind what you were doing, underneath everything that was happening, God was doing something good. God was making everything right again."

Joseph didn't punish them, he rescued them — he brought God's special family to live safely with him in Egypt.

One day, God would send another Prince, a young Prince whose heart would break. Like Joseph, he would leave his home and his Father. His brothers would hate him and want him dead. He would be sold for pieces of silver. He would be punished even though he had done nothing wrong.

But God would use everything that
happened to this young Prince — even
the bad things — to do something good:
to forgive the sins of the whole world.

God to the rescue!

Moses and the Great Escape from Egypt, from Exodus 3 – 13

JOSEPH AND HIS BROTHERS grew old and died, but their children's children stayed on in Egypt where they became a very LARGE family.

Later on, a new king began to rule, but this pharaoh didn't remember Joseph and he didn't like God's people. He made them into his slaves and beat them and made them work harder and harder.

God's people cried out to God to rescue them.

And God heard them. He remembered his promise to Abraham. He would look after his people. He would find a way to set them free.

One day, Moses was looking after sheep when something caught his eye: a bush was behaving very oddly — it was flickering with flames, but its leaves weren't burning up. He took a closer look.

"Moses!" boomed a big voice.

Moses leapt back. The bush was talking to him!

"I have heard my people's cries," God said. "I have seen their tears. So I have come down to rescue them. Go to Pharaoh and tell him to let my people go free."

Moses was afraid. But God said, "I will be with you."

So Moses went to Pharaoh.

"Pharaoh," Moses began, "God says — "

"God?" said Pharaoh. "Never heard of him."

Moses kept going. "God says, let his people go free."

"Why should I?" Pharaoh said. "Don't want to. WON'T!" So he didn't.

So God gave Pharaoh ten warnings, called "Plagues."

First, God turned the River Nile into blood. No one could drink the water. But still Pharaoh would not let them go.

So God made frogs come hopping and leaping and jumping. In your bed frogs, in your hair frogs, in your soup frogs, all over everywhere frogs! "Make them go away!" Pharaoh screamed. "Then your people can go." So God took the frogs away.

But Pharaoh changed his mind. "You can't go!" he said.

Then God sent zillions of gnats. But still Pharaoh said, "NO!" So then God sent swarms of flies — flies buzzing in your eyes flies.

And after that, sickness; and horrible boils; and huge hailstones; and a storm of locusts; then darkness when it should have been day — until it seemed that the whole world, creation and everything, was coming undone, falling back into darkness. And emptiness. And nothingness.

But each time Pharaoh said, "Make it stop and then I'll let them go!" And each time when God made it stop, Pharaoh changed his mind and said, "Actually, NO! You can't go!"

Finally, Moses warned Pharaoh, "Obey God or he will have to send the worst thing of all." Pharaoh just laughed.

So God said, "The oldest boy in each family of Egypt must die. But my people will be safe."

God told his people to take their best lamb, to kill it and to put some of its blood on their front doors. "When God passes over your house," Moses explained, "God will see the blood and know that the lamb died instead of you."

That night, it was just as God had said. Suddenly, piercing the darkness, echoing down the corridors of the palace, came a blood-curdling scream. Pharaoh's oldest son had died! At last, Pharaoh did what God said. "GET OUT!" Pharaoh shouted. "JUST GO!"

And so, that very night, Moses and God's people fled out of Egypt and out of slavery. They were free at last!

God's people would always remember this great rescue and call it "Passover." But an even Greater Rescue was coming.

Many years later, God was going to do it again. He was going to come down once more to rescue his people. But this time God was going to set them free forever and ever.

God makes a way

Moses and the Red Sea,
from Exodus 14–15

MOSES AND GOD'S people
escaped out of Egypt and into the
wilderness. They didn't know the way — but God knew
the way and he would show them.

"I will bring you to a new home, a special land," God
promised them. "I will look after you. I am with you."

God sent a big cloud for them to follow — a pillar of
smoke stretching up to the sky. It moved in front of them as
they walked and shaded them from the blazing heat of the
day. And when it was time to rest, it stopped. All through
the cold desert nights it kept them warm, glowing like fire.

God led his people through the desert to the edge of a
great sea. They were just wondering how to cross it when,
suddenly, they heard a terrible thundering and pounding.
It sounded almost like horses' hooves. They shaded their
eyes to look back — and screamed! It was! Pharaoh and
his army were coming to get them!

Pharaoh had changed his mind again. "Get my slaves
BACK!" he screeched and charged out into the desert
after them — with 600 of his fastest horsemen — and
every single chariot in Egypt.

What were God's people going to do? In front of them was a big sea. It was so big there was no way around it. But there was no way through it — it was too deep. They didn't have any boats so they couldn't sail across. And they couldn't swim across because it was too far and they would drown. And they couldn't turn back because Pharaoh was chasing them. They could see the flashing swords now, glinting in the baking sun, and the dust clouds, and chariot after scary chariot surging towards them. So they did the only thing there was left to do — PANIC!

"We're going to die!" they shrieked.

"Don't be afraid!" Moses said.

"But there's nothing we can do!" they screamed.

"God knows you can't do anything!" Moses said. "God will do it for you. Trust him. And watch!"

"But there's no way out!" they cried.

"God will make a way!" Moses said.

Another minute and it would have been over. But then the strangest thing happened.

God made the pillar of smoke move. It moved behind his people and hid them from the Egyptians. Then God sent a strong east wind to blow all night long. It blew on the water of the big sea. It blew it to the left and it blew it to the right, until it blew it into two towering walls of water, and there — right through the middle of the sea — a muddy pathway opened up.

And God's people walked across on dry land!

When the Egyptians tried to follow, the walls of water crashed back down on them and swallowed them up.

God's people were safe. They danced and laughed and sang and thanked God — when there had been no way out, God had made a way.

Many years later, once again, God was going to make a way where there was no way.

From the beginning, God's children had been running from him and hiding. God knew his children could never be happy without him. But they couldn't get back to him by themselves — they were lost, they didn't know the way back.

But God knew the way.

And one day he would show them.

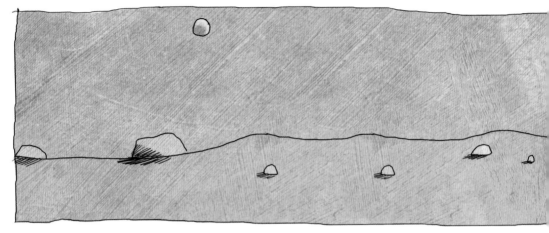

Ten ways to be perfect

Moses and the Ten Commandments, from Exodus 16 – 17, 19 – 40

SO THERE THEY all were. Grannies, granddads, babies, uncles, aunts, children, moms, and dads. Out there in the middle of the desert. They had blisters from all the walking. They were hungry. And thirsty. And much, much too hot.

"We don't like it!" they said. "It stinks!"(And so did they, for that matter, because no one had taken a bath in weeks.)

Now remember — because this is something they'd forgotten — God had done amazing things for his people. He'd hidden them inside a cloud. He'd moved the sea. He'd set them free.

But God's people still weren't happy. They didn't care about being free — wasn't it better when they were slaves? At least they'd had lots of nice food to eat.

"God doesn't want us to be happy," they said. It was the same lie that Adam and Eve had heard all those years before. "God has brought us out here to kill us. God doesn't love us!" But they didn't know God very well, did they?

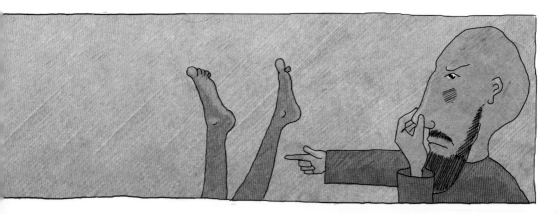

Every day of their journey, God kept on showing his people how well he would look after them, if they would trust him, and obey him. When they were hungry, God made the sky rain with food — bread coming down from heaven! "What is it?" they asked each other. They didn't know, so they called it, "What is it?" (which, of course, is a very good name for something when you don't know what it is). When they were thirsty and started quarrelling, God made water flow from a rock. Moses called that place "Quarrelling" (because that seemed like a good name, too).

And still God's children didn't trust him or do what he said. They thought they could do a better job of looking after themselves and making themselves happy. But God knew there was no such thing as happiness without him.

So God led them to a tall mountain. God wanted to talk to his people and show them what he was like. He wanted to help them know him better and tell them about the special land he was going to give them.

"The whole earth belongs to me!" God said. "But I have chosen you — you are my special family. I want you to live in a way that shows everyone else what I'm like — so they can know me, too."

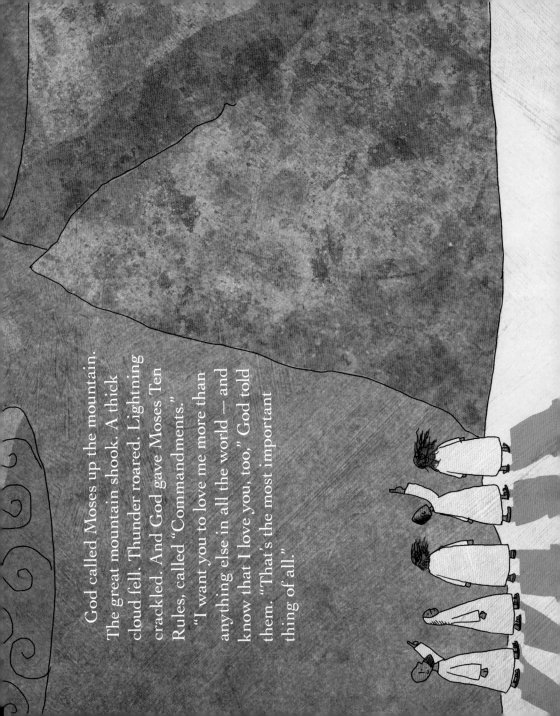

God called Moses up the mountain. The great mountain shook. A thick cloud fell. Thunder roared. Lightning crackled. And God gave Moses Ten Rules, called "Commandments."

"I want you to love me more than anything else in all the world — and know that I love you, too," God told them. "That's the most important thing of all."

God gave them other rules, like don't make yourselves pretend gods; don't kill people; or steal; or lie. The rules showed God's people how to live, and how to be close to him, and how to be happy. They showed how life worked best.

"God promises to always look after you," Moses said. "Will you love him and keep these rules?"

"We can do it! Yes! We promise!"

But they were wrong. They couldn't do it. No matter how hard they tried, they could never keep God's rules all the time.

God knew they couldn't. And he wanted them to know it, too.

Only one Person could keep all the rules. And many years later God would send him — to stand in their place and be perfect for them.

Because the rules couldn't save them.

Only God could save them.

The warrior leader

Joshua and the battle of Jericho, from Joshua 3 and 6

AFTER MOSES DIED, God gave his people a new leader. His name was Joshua, which means "The Lord Saves." Joshua was going to lead God's people into the special land God had promised to give them.

By this time, God's people had been wandering around in that baking desert for 40 years! So you can imagine how sick they were of sand and anything yellow and tents and walking and being hot. And how happy they were to reach the edge of the desert and to see their beautiful new home — right there in front of them — all cool and green and lovely. There was only one problem.

Jericho.

Jericho was a city — but it wasn't just any old city. It was a fortress and it stopped anyone from getting into the land.

The people looked at Jericho. At the big, giant, scary walls all around it. At the tall towering ramparts. At the heavy iron gates bolted shut. At each other.

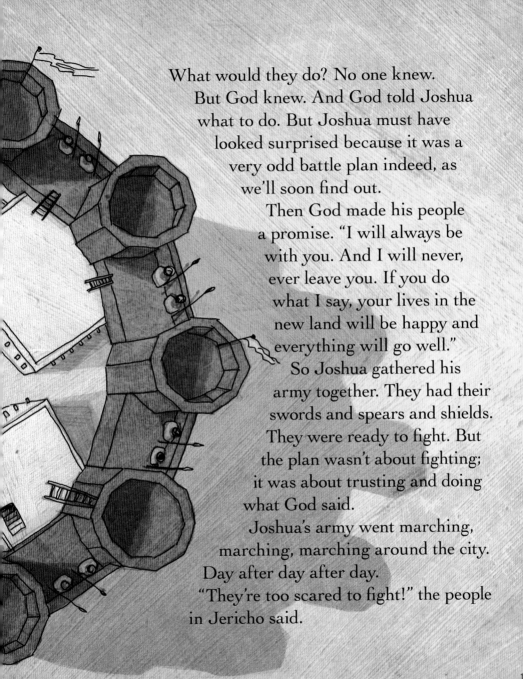

What would they do? No one knew.
But God knew. And God told Joshua
what to do. But Joshua must have
looked surprised because it was a
very odd battle plan indeed, as
we'll soon find out.

Then God made his people
a promise. "I will always be
with you. And I will never,
ever leave you. If you do
what I say, your lives in the
new land will be happy and
everything will go well."

So Joshua gathered his
army together. They had their
swords and spears and shields.
They were ready to fight. But
the plan wasn't about fighting;
it was about trusting and doing
what God said.

Joshua's army went marching,
marching, marching around the city.
Day after day after day.

"They're too scared to fight!" the people
in Jericho said.

But they were wrong. God's people weren't scared — they were waiting. Waiting for God to tell them what to do next.

On the seventh day, God told his people to march around the city not once, but seven times. Then God told everyone to make as much noise as they could. (Has anyone ever told you to make as much noise as you possibly can? Well, imagine that noise, add 39,999 other people making that noise, too — and you get the idea. Ear-splitting!)

And, as it turned out, stone-splitting, too — because the huge, strong walls of Jericho just crumbled to the ground, as if they were made of sand. Jericho vanished in a great cloud of dust.

So it was that God's people entered their new home. And they didn't have to fight to get in — they only had to walk.

Joshua said, "God has brought you safely here. Now will you do what he says?"

Everyone said, "We promise!"

"Only God can make your heart happy," Joshua said. "So don't pray to pretend gods."

"No," they said. "Never!"

I'm afraid they didn't keep their promise. They didn't do what God said and many years later, just as God warned them, things would go badly for God's people. They would lose their home. Enemies would capture them and take them off as slaves. And God's people would scatter into many different lands.

But God's Plan was still working.

One day he would give his people another Leader. And another home.

But this home, no one could ever take from them.

The teeny, weenie ... true king

Samuel anoints David, from 1 Samuel 16

GOD'S PEOPLE had a new land. Now they wanted a king.

"But God is your King," Samuel told them. "He is the one who looks after you best."

"We want a real king!" they said. "One we can see!"

God knew that a king might not be kind to his people or look after them as well as he would. But God's people didn't care; they wanted a king and they wanted him now!

So God gave them a king.

He was called Saul and he seemed like a good king — at first. But he became proud and stopped listening to God. He didn't obey God. Or love God with his whole heart.

"Saul can't help me with my plan," God said.

"I need a king who loves me and will teach my people to love me. I need a true king." God had just the one in mind.

"Go to Bethlehem," God told Samuel. "You'll find the new king there." (Samuel's job was to listen to God and tell people what God said.)

So Samuel went to the little town of Bethlehem. God told Samuel to go to Jesse's house. God was going to choose one of Jesse's sons to be the new king.

Jesse had seven strong sons.

Now in those days if you were going to be the king, you didn't have to be the richest or the cleverest (although that was always nice). You had to look like a king, which meant you had to be the tallest and the strongest. (So you could carry the longest swords and biggest armor and defeat everyone.) And it didn't hurt to be handsome, either.

Samuel asked Jesse to bring him each son in turn.
So Jesse brought the oldest, tallest, strongest son. *This must be the new king*, Samuel thought. *He looks like a king.*

But God didn't choose him. "You're thinking about what he looks like on the outside," God told Samuel. "But I am looking at his heart, what he's like on the inside."

So Jesse showed Samuel his next oldest, tallest, strongest son. But God didn't choose him either. In fact, God didn't choose any of the seven sons.

Samuel said, "Is that all?"

Jesse laughed. "Oh, well, there's the youngest one, but he's just the weakling of the family, he's only teeny —"

"Bring him," said Samuel.

Jesse's youngest son came running up, and God spoke quietly to Samuel, "This is the one!"

His name was David.

"He has a heart like mine," God said. "It is full of love. He will help me with my Secret Rescue Plan. And one of his children's children's children will be the King. And that King will rule the world forever."

Samuel anointed David's head with oil — which was a special way to show that you are God's chosen king. "You will be the new king one day," Samuel told him.

And, sure enough, when he grew up, David became king.

God chose David to be king because God was getting his people ready for an even greater King who was coming.

Once again, God would say, "Go to Bethlehem. You'll find the new King there." And there, one starry night in Bethlehem, in the town of David, three Wise Men would find him.

The young hero and
the horrible giant

David and Goliath, from 1 Samuel 17

GOD'S PEOPLE HAD SOME scary enemies, but the Philistines were the scariest of them all. And now the Philistines had come to fight them.

The Philistines had a secret weapon, called "Goliath." Goliath was a terrifying soldier, and — worst of all — a GIANT! A giant so strong, and so tall, and so scary that no one had ever been able to fight him — and live to tell the tale.

So, there they were: the Philistines standing on the top of one hill; God's people standing on top of the other. Every day, Goliath came out and shouted, "Send your best soldier to fight me! If he wins, we will be your slaves. But if I win, you will be our slaves!" No one spoke. No one moved.

"Chickens!" Goliath bellowed. "Your God can't save you! I'll rip your heads off and have you on toast!" His beady, greedy eyes glowered at them hungrily from under his horrible helmet — as if any minute he really might just gobble them all up. And he laughed his terrible laugh. "Ha-Ha-Ha-Ha" it boomed, echoing horribly around and around the dry, dry valley.

Well, Goliath might just as well have been a green, slimy monster with three heads because God's people froze with fear. Their eyes glazed over, and they turned deathly pale. They knew if someone didn't do something quick, if someone didn't save them —

But God would do something. He would send someone to save them.

Now, you remember that David was the youngest son of Jesse? Well his brothers were soldiers in the army. One day, when David brought his brothers their lunches, he saw Goliath — and he saw how scared everyone was.

"Don't be afraid!" David said. "I'll fight him for you!"

"You're only a little shepherd boy," the king said, "and Goliath is a great soldier. How will you fight him?"

"God will help me!" David said.

So the king gave David his royal armor to wear, but it was too heavy and too big and David couldn't even walk. "I won't need this," David said.

Instead, David picked out five smooth stones from the stream — one, two, three, four, five — took his slingshot and walked towards Goliath. Step. Step. Step.

Goliath walked towards David. THUD. THUD. THUD. "You?" Goliath peered down at the small boy. "I'm little!" David shouted up to him. "But God is great!"

Goliath laughed an even terribler laugh than usual. "HAAAA-HA-HA-HAAAA!" it went. With just one swing of his giant sword, Goliath could finish the boy off.

But David kept going. "It isn't how strong you are or how many swords and spears you have that will save you — it is God who saves you! This is God's battle. And God always wins his battles!"

David put a stone in his sling, swung it around — and let it go. The little stone flew WHIZZ like a bullet through the air and struck Goliath THUD right between the eyes. Goliath stopped laughing …

He stumbled … and staggered … and CRASH! fell dead.
When the Philistines saw Goliath was dead, they ran
away. And when God's people saw them running away,
they cheered. God had saved his people. David was a hero!

Many years later, God would send his people another young Hero to fight for them. And to save them.

But this Hero would fight the greatest battle the world has ever known.

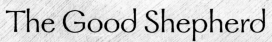

The Good Shepherd

*David the Shepherd King, from Psalm 51, 2 Samuel 7;
paraphrase of Psalm 23*

DAVID WAS A SHEPHERD, but when God looked at him, he saw a king.

Sure enough, when David grew up, that's just what he became. And David was a great king. He had a heart like God's heart — full of love.

Now, that didn't mean he was perfect, because he did some terrible things — he even murdered a man. No, David made a big mess of his life. But God can take even the biggest mess and make it work in his plan.

"I need a new heart, Lord," David prayed, "because mine is full of sin. Make me clean inside."

God heard David's prayer. He forgave David and he made David a promise: "I will make you great, David. And one day, a King will be born into your family, and he will heal the whole world."

Did you know that David was a songwriter, too? In fact his songs were so good, they might have been in the top 40 charts (if they'd been invented then).

David's songs are like prayers. They are called psalms and this one is called "The Song of the Shepherd." (It's probably number one on the Psalm Charts.) And it goes like this ...

131

God is my Shepherd
And I am his little lamb.

He feeds me
He guides me
He looks after me.
I have everything I need.

Inside, my heart is very quiet.
As quiet as lying still in soft green grass
In a meadow
By a little stream.

Even when I walk through
the dark, scary, lonely places
I won't be afraid
Because my Shepherd knows where I am.

He is here with me
He keeps me safe
He rescues me

He makes me strong
And brave.

He is getting wonderful things ready for me
Especially for me
Everything I ever dreamed of!

He fills my heart so full of happiness
I can't hold it all inside.

Wherever I go I know
God's Never Stopping
Never Giving Up
Unbreaking
Always and Forever
Love
Will go, too!

God gave David that song to sing to his people, so they could know that he loved them and would always look after them — like a shepherd loves his sheep.

And one day, God was going to do something that would inspire thousands upon thousands of new songs. God was going to show his people once and for all just how much he loved them.

Another Shepherd was coming — a greater Shepherd. He would be called the Good Shepherd. And this Shepherd was going to lead all of God's lambs back to the place where they had always belonged — close to God's heart.

A little servant girl
and the proud general

The little slave girl and Naaman, from 2 Kings 5

NAAMAN WAS a very important man in a very important army of a very important country. So you see, he was
very, very, very important.

But Naaman was sick. He had leprosy, which is a nasty
thing that stops you from feeling anything. Bits of you

fall off without you noticing, like bashed fingers and squished toes. It might sound funny but it wasn't — and Naaman certainly wasn't laughing. There was no cure, it never went away, and in the end it killed you. Naaman needed help.

Now there was a little slave girl who worked for Naaman and she knew someone who could help him. But there was a problem; Naaman was her enemy.

Not long before, Naaman had led an army raid on her home in Israel. He had killed her whole family, carried her off to Syria, and made her into his slave. Every night she cried herself to sleep — she had lost everything.

Why would she, of all people, want to help Naaman? Didn't she hate him and want to hurt him back? Didn't she want to make him pay for the wrong he'd done?

That's what you would expect, but instead of hating him, she loved him. Instead of hurting him back, she forgave him.

"I want Naaman to get well," she said to her mistress. "There's a man in Israel called Elisha who can heal him."

"I'll go," said Naaman, loading up his wagons and putting on his flashing armor. "But I'll go to the palace because that's where someone important like me gets healed!"

So he hurried off to Israel and went straight to the king. "My healing, please!" he announced.

"I can do lots of things!" the king replied. "But only God can heal."

Just then a message from Elisha arrived. "Send Naaman here," it read.

So Namaan hurried off to Elisha's house. But Elisha didn't even come out and greet him, he just sent a servant instead. *Doesn't Elisha realize who I am?* Naaman thought.

But what the servant said next made him even crosser. "Wash in there!" he said.

"Just wash?" Naaman laughed. "In that slimy, stinky river?" He looked around to see if this was some kind of joke. It wasn't. *Any person can wash in a river!* he thought. *I am Naaman. I am important. I should do something important so God will heal me!* And he rode off in a rage. (Of course, you and I both know, that's not how God does things. All Naaman needed was nothing. It was the one thing Naaman didn't have.)

God knew that Naaman was even sicker on the inside than he was on the outside. Naaman was proud. He thought he didn't need God. His heart didn't work properly — it couldn't feel anything. You see, Naaman had leprosy of his heart. God was not only going to heal Naaman's skin, he was going to heal his pride.

Naaman finally agreed to wash in the river, and instantly, his skin became smooth like a baby.

Naaman wanted to pay Elisha.

"God healed you. You can't pay," Elisha said. "It's free."

And so it was that a very sick man was healed — all because of a little servant girl who forgave him.

God knew sin was like leprosy. It stopped his children's hearts from working properly and in the end it would kill them. Years later, God was going to send another Servant, to forgive as she did — to forgive all of God's children and heal the terrible sickness in their hearts.

Their hearts were broken.

But God can mend broken hearts.

Operation "No More Tears!"

The Rescuer will come: prophecies from
Isaiah 9, 11, 40, 50, 53, 55, 60

DO YOU KNOW what your name means? Well, there was once a man called Isaiah, and his name meant "God to the rescue!"

That might sound like a bit of a funny name to you, but it was just the right name for Isaiah because God had a special job for Isaiah. You see, Isaiah's job was to listen to God and then tell people what he heard.

Now, God let Isaiah know a secret. God was going to mend his broken world. He showed Isaiah his Secret Rescue Plan: Operation "No More Tears!"

This is the message God gave Isaiah (it was like a letter God wrote to his children) . . .

Dear Little Flock,

You're all wandering away from me,
like sheep in an open field. You have always
been running away from me. And now you're
lost. You can't find your way back.
But I can't stop loving you. I will come to find you.
So I am sending you a Shepherd to look after you
and love you. To carry you home to me.

You've been stumbling around, like people in a dark room. But into the darkness, a bright Light will shine! It will chase away all the shadows, like sunshine.

A little baby will be born. A Royal Son. His mommy will be a young girl who doesn't have a husband. His name will be Emmanuel, which means "God has come to live with us." He is one of King David's children's children's children.

The Prince of Peace.

Yes, Someone is going to come and rescue you!

But he won't be who anyone expects.

He will be a King! But he won't live in a palace. And he won't have lots of money. He will be poor. And he will be a Servant. But this King will heal the whole world.

He will be a Hero! He will fight for his people, and rescue them from their enemies. But he won't have big armies, and he won't fight with swords.

He will make the blind see, he will make the lame leap like deer! He will make everything the way it was always meant to be. But people will hate him, and they won't listen to him. He will be like a Lamb — he will suffer and die.

It's the Secret Rescue Plan we made – from before the beginning of the world!

It's the only way to get you back.

But he won't stay dead – I will make him alive again!

And, one day, when he comes back to rule forever, the mountains and trees will dance and sing for joy! The earth will shout out loud! His fame will fill the whole earth – as the waters cover the sea! Everything sad will come untrue. Even death is going to die! And he will wipe away every tear from every eye.

Yes, the Rescuer will come. Look for him.

Wait for him. He will come!

I promise.

Poor Isaiah. He read God's letter over and over to God's people, but no one listened to him — at all. Ever. They didn't want to hear God's promise. They didn't believe it.

Did it sound maybe too good to be true? A story that ends happily ever after? Well, it does sound like a fairy tale, doesn't it? And, as anyone will quickly tell you, fairy tales aren't true.

Or are they?

Daniel and the scary sleepover

Daniel and the lions' den, from Daniel 6

THINGS WERE NOT looking good for God's people. They had been captured and taken far from home — and now they were slaves of the king of Babylon. But God had not left his people. He was with them and he was looking after them. Daniel loved God and obeyed him. Now God made Daniel able to understand lots of difficult things, so it wasn't long before the king of Babylon noticed him. King Darius liked how clever Daniel was. So he made Daniel his most important helper of all, and put him in charge of lots of other helpers.

But the other helpers didn't like this. They wanted the king to like them best. They wanted to get rid of Daniel.

So they spied on Daniel. They tried to find things wrong with Daniel, things they could tell the king, things they could ... but there weren't any. None. They couldn't find anything at all.

Except there was just the one thing: every day, three times a day — without fail, no matter what — Daniel went to his room, closed the door, and prayed.

They smiled to themselves. "Let's get the king to make a law — no one is allowed to pray to anyone EXCEPT TO THE KING! Daniel won't obey this law and he will be punished!"

They were pleased with themselves for being so clever and hurried off to tell the king. The king liked their idea. He didn't know they were tricking him. So he made it into a law: "Everyone must pray — only to ME! If you don't, the lions will have you for their dinner!"

Daniel heard this. He knew it was wrong to pray to anyone except God. He had to do what God said — whatever it cost him, even if it meant he would die. So Daniel went to his room, closed the door, and prayed.

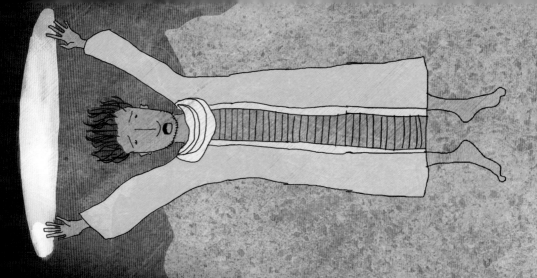

That's just what the bad men knew Daniel would do. They skipped straight off to tell the king. "Oh, Your Most Glittering Highness, your law says, does it not, that everyone must pray to you alone, Sire?"

"Yes," said the king.

"Oh, Majesterial Brightness, then correct us if we're wrong but . . . it would seem that Daniel is praying to God — NOT TO YOU!"

The king was sad. He had been tricked! He didn't want to hurt Daniel, but he couldn't change his law. And so he let the soldiers throw Daniel to the lions. "May your God, who you love so much, rescue you!" the king said.

The king went back to his palace, but he didn't sleep that night. Not a wink. He tossed and turned until finally, at the first glimmer of dawn, he leaped out of bed and ran straight to the den. "Daniel?" he cried. "Has your God rescued you?"

"YES!" Daniel shouted. "God sent an angel to close the lions' mouths!"

And there, resting his head on Daniel's lap, was the biggest lion, purring like a little kitten.

The king brought Daniel out of the den. "Look!" he said. "Daniel doesn't even have a scratch!"

The king made a new law: "Daniel's God is the true God. The God who Rescues! Pray to him instead!"

God would keep on rescuing his people. And the time was coming when God would send another brave Hero, like Daniel, who would love God and do what God said — whatever it cost him, even if it meant he would die.

And together they would pull off the Greatest Rescue the world has ever known.

God's messenger

Jonah and the big fish, from Jonah 1 – 4; Hebrews 1:1 – 2

GOD HAD A JOB for Jonah. But Jonah didn't want it.

"Go to Nineveh," God said, "and tell your worst enemies that I love them."

"NO!" said Jonah. "Those are bad people doing bad things!"

"Exactly," said God. "They have run far away from me. But I can't stop loving them. I will give them a new start. I will forgive them."

"NO!" said Jonah. "They don't deserve it!"

I'll run away! Jonah said to himself. *Far away — so far away that God won't be able to find me. Then I won't have to do what God says! It's a good plan!* he said, because, as far as he knew, it was a good plan.

But, of course, it wasn't a good plan at all. It was a silly plan. (Because you can run away from God, but he will always come and find you.)

Jonah went ahead with his not-very-good plan. "One ticket to NOT Nineveh, please!" he said and boarded a boat sailing in the very opposite direction of Nineveh.

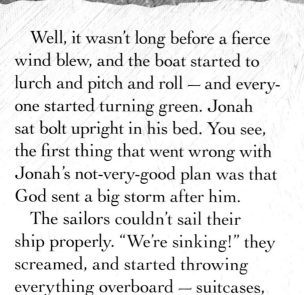

Well, it wasn't long before a fierce wind blew, and the boat started to lurch and pitch and roll — and everyone started turning green. Jonah sat bolt upright in his bed. You see, the first thing that went wrong with Jonah's not-very-good plan was that God sent a big storm after him.

The sailors couldn't sail their ship properly. "We're sinking!" they screamed, and started throwing everything overboard — suitcases, food, whatever they could find.

By now Jonah knew that the storm was his fault. "Throw me in, instead!" he shouted to the sailors. "And the storm will stop!" The sailors weren't sure. "It's the only way you can be saved!" Jonah cried.

And so, one ... two ... three ...

163

SPLASH!
No sooner had Jonah hit the water than the waves grew calm, the wind died down, and the storm stopped.

Just then, when Jonah thought it was all over, when he was sure he was going to drown, God sent a big fish to rescue him. The fish swallowed Jonah whole — with one big gulp.

Jonah must have thought he'd died, it was so dark in there, like in a tomb. But then he smelled the rotting food and felt the slimy seaweed and knew he wasn't dead. He was in the belly of the fish!

Sitting there in the darkness for three whole days, Jonah had plenty of time to think. Pretty soon he realized his plan was, well … a very silly plan indeed. He was sorry for running away. He prayed to God from inside the great fish and asked God to forgive him.

After three days, the fish spat Jonah safely out onto a sandy beach.

Just then, Jonah heard someone calling his name. "Go to Nineveh," God said.

And this time? Jonah said, "YES!" He went straight to Nineveh and told everyone God's wonderful message.

"Even though you've run far from God, he can't stop loving you," Jonah told them. "Run to him! So he can forgive you."

The people of Nineveh listened to Jonah, and they started loving God. They learned to do what God said and to stop running away from him — just like Jonah.

Many years later, God was going to send another Messenger with the same wonderful message. Like Jonah, he would spend three days in utter darkness.

But this Messenger would be God's own Son. He would be called "The Word" because he himself would be God's Message. God's Message translated into our own language. Everything God wanted to say to the whole world — in a Person.

Get ready!

God's people return from being slaves,
from Nehemiah 8 – 10, Malachi 1, 3 and 4, Ezra 7

HAVE YOU EVER been to a party that lasted a whole week? How about a sermon that went on all day?

Well, that's what happened to God's people after they came home from being slaves. They had forgotten how God wanted them to live, or who they were supposed to be. So Ezra and Nehemiah read them the rules God had given Moses.

But something odd happened: the more the sermon went on, the sadder they all got. Why? Was the sermon that boring? No, not really. It was strange, you see. As Ezra read the book of rules, it worked like a mirror. It showed them what they were like, and they didn't like

* Rules
* More rules
* Even more rules
* Yet more rules
* Bonus rules
* More and more rules
* Rules about the rules
* Bonus supplementary rules
* More supplementary rules
* Rules and rules
* Additional rules
* Ancillary rules
* Plus some other rules
* Rules and further rules
* A couple of added rul...
* Extra extra more r...
* Plus further other...
* Rules, rules, and...

what they saw. They saw that they had not been living the way they should. They saw that they were cruel and selfish.

"We've blown it," they cried. "Now God will punish us!"

They thought they knew what God was going to do. But they didn't. Of course, they might have picked up a clue from Ezra's name, which means "Help is here!" And an even stronger one from Nehemiah's name, because his name means "God wipes away our tears." And that, as you'll see, is just exactly what God was getting ready to do.

Ezra looked at God's children. Great, hot tears were welling up in their eyes and streaming down their cheeks. He stopped his sermon — mid-sentence — and shut the book. "We're having a party!" he shouted.

And so that's just what they did! All week long.

"God wants us to be happy," Ezra said.

All day they listened to stories about the wonderful things God had done for his people. How he made the world. How he gave a special promise to Abraham. How he rescued them from slavery. How he spoke to Moses and showed them how to live. How he brought them to a special land. How he rescued them — no matter what, time after time, over and over again — because of his

Never Stopping, Never Giving Up, Unbreaking, Always and Forever Love.

They remembered how God had always, all through the years, been loving his children — keeping his promise to Abraham, taking care of them, forgiving them. Even when they disobeyed. Even when they ran away from him. Even when they thought they didn't need him.

Then God told his children something more ...

I can't stop loving you.
You are my heart's treasure.
But I lost you.
Now I am coming back for you.

I am like the sun that gently shines on you,
chasing away darkness and fear and death.
You'll be so happy —
you'll be like little calves running free
in an open field.

I am going to send my Messenger —The Promised One.
The One you have been waiting for.
The Rescuer.

He is coming. So, get ready!

It had taken centuries for God's people to be ready, but now the time had almost come for the best part of God's Plan.

God himself was going to come. Not to punish his people — but to rescue them.

God was getting ready to wipe away every tear from every eye.

And the true party was just about to begin . . .

He's here!

The Nativity, from Luke 1 – 2

EVERYTHING WAS READY. The moment God had been waiting for was here at last! God was coming to help his people, just as he promised in the beginning.

But how would he come? What would he be like? What would he do?

Mountains would have bowed down. Seas would have roared. Trees would have clapped their hands. But the earth held its breath. As silent as snow falling, he came in. And when no one was looking, in the darkness, he came.

There was a young girl who was engaged to a man named Joseph. (Joseph was the great-great-great-great-great grandson of King David.)

One morning, this girl was minding her own business when, suddenly, a great warrior of light appeared — right there, in her bedroom. He was Gabriel and he was an angel, a special messenger from heaven.

When she saw the tall shining man standing there, Mary was frightened.

"You don't need to be scared," Gabriel said. "God is very happy with you!"

Mary looked around to see if perhaps he was talking to someone else.

"Mary," Gabriel said, and he laughed with such gladness that Mary's eyes filled with sudden tears.

"Mary, you're going to have a baby. A little boy. You will call him Jesus. He is God's own Son. He's the One! He's the Rescuer!"

The God who flung planets into space and kept them whirling around and around, the God who made the universe with just a word, the one who could do anything at all — was making himself small. And coming down … as a baby.

Wait. God was sending a baby to rescue the world?

"But it's too wonderful!" Mary said and felt her heart beating hard. "How can it be true?"

"Is anything too wonderful for God?" Gabriel asked.

So Mary trusted God more than what her eyes could see. And she believed. "I am God's servant," she said. "Whatever God says, I will do."

Sure enough, it was just as the angel had said. Nine months later, Mary was almost ready to have her baby.

Now, Mary and Joseph had to take a trip to Bethlehem, the town King David was from. But when they reached the little town, they found every room was full. Every bed was taken.

"Go away!" the innkeepers told them. "There isn't any place for you."

Where would they stay? Soon Mary's baby would come.

They couldn't find anywhere except an old, tumbledown stable. So they stayed where the cows and the donkeys and the horses stayed.

And there, in the stable, amongst the chickens and the donkeys and the cows, in the quiet of the night, God gave the world his wonderful gift. The baby that would change the world was born. His baby Son.

Mary and Joseph wrapped him up to keep him warm. They made a soft bed of straw and used the animals' feeding trough as his cradle. And they gazed in wonder at God's Great Gift, wrapped in swaddling clothes, and lying in a manger.

Mary and Joseph named him Jesus, "Emmanuel" — which means "God has come to live with us."

Because, of course, he had.

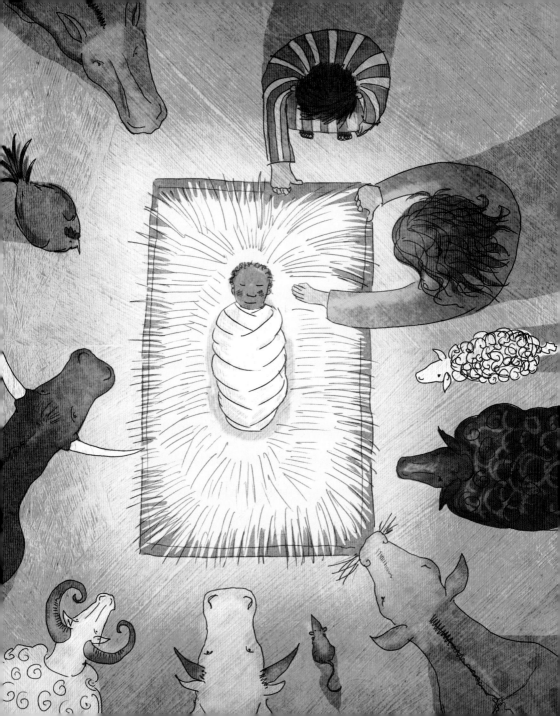

The Light of the whole world

The story of the shepherds, from Luke 2

THAT SAME NIGHT, in amongst the other stars, suddenly a bright new star appeared. Of all the stars in the dark vaulted heavens, this one shone clearer. It blazed in the night and made the other stars look pale beside it.

God put it there when his baby Son was born — to be like a spotlight. Shining on him. Lighting up the darkness. Showing people the way to him.

You see, God was like a new daddy — he couldn't keep the good news to himself. He'd been waiting all these long years for this moment, and now he wanted to tell everyone.

So he pulled out all the stops. He'd sent an angel to tell Mary the good news. He'd put a special star in the sky to show where his boy was. And now he was going to send a big choir of angels to sing his happy song to the world: *He's here! He's come! Go and see him. My little Boy.*

Now where would you send your splendid choir? To a big concert hall maybe? Or a palace perhaps? God sent his to a little hillside, outside a little town, in the middle of the night. He sent all those angels to sing for a raggedy old bunch of shepherds watching their sheep outside Bethlehem.

In those days, remember, people used to laugh at shepherds and say they were smelly and call them other rude names (which I can't possibly mention here). You see, people thought shepherds were no-bodies, just scruffy old riff-raff.

But God must have thought shepherds were very important indeed, because they're the ones he chose to tell the good news to first.

That night some shepherds were out in the open fields, warming themselves by a campfire, when suddenly the sheep darted. They were frightened by something. The olive trees rustled. What was that... A wing beat?

They turned around. Standing in front of them was a huge warrior of light, blazing in the darkness. "Don't be afraid of me!" the bright shining man said. "I haven't come to hurt you. I've come to bring you happy news for everyone everywhere. Today, in David's town, in Bethlehem, God's Son has been born! You can go and see him. He is sleeping in a manger."

Behind the angel they saw a strange glowing cloud — except it wasn't a cloud, it was angels . . . troops and troops of angels, armed with light! And they were singing a beautiful song: "Glory to God! To God be Fame and Honor and all our Hoorays!"

Then as quickly as they appeared, the angels left.

The shepherds stamped out their fire, left their sheep, raced down the grassy hill, through the gates of Bethlehem, down the narrow cobble streets, through a courtyard, down some step, step, steps, past an inn, round a corner, through a hedge, until, at last, they reached . . .

a tumbledown stable.

They caught their breath. Then quietly, they tiptoed inside.

They knelt on the dirt floor. They had heard about this Promised Child and now he was here. Heaven's Son. The Maker of the Stars. A baby sleeping in his mother's arms.

This baby would be like that bright star shining in the sky that night. A Light to light up the whole world. Chasing away darkness. Helping people to see.

And the darker the night got, the brighter the star would shine.

The King of all kings

The story of the three Wise Men, from Matthew 2

FAR AWAY, in the East, three clever men saw the very same star. The star that God had put in the sky when Jesus was born. They knew it was a sign. A baby king had been born.

They had been waiting for this star. They knew it would come.

"He's here!" they shouted. "He's here!" (And I'm sure if you'd been there, you would have heard them laughing and dancing and singing until the sun came up!)

At dawn, they packed up their camels and wrapped gifts for the baby. They brought their most precious treasures of all: frankincense, gold, and myrrh. Special, sparkly, lovely-smelling, gleaming things — just right for a king.

The three Wise Men (actually, if you'd met them, you'd have thought they were kings because they were so rich and clever and important looking) set off.

They rode their camels ...

Across endless deserts ...

Up steep, steep mountains ...

Down into deep, deep valleys …

Through raging rivers …

Over grassy plains …

night and day, and day and night, for hours that turned into days, that turned into weeks, that turned into months and months, until, at last, they reached …

Jerusalem.

Jerusalem was by far the most important city for miles around and, as anyone can tell you, that's where a palace would be and kings are born in palaces. So that's where they went. But they were in for a surprise.

They went to see King Herod. Surely he'd know where this baby was.

But he didn't. In fact, he didn't like the sound of a new king — it made him cross. He didn't want anyone to be king, except him.

But Herod's advisors told the three Wise Men what was written in their books — what God had said about the baby king: "Go to Bethlehem. That's where you'll find him."

Suddenly the star they had seen in the East started moving again, showing them the way. So the three Wise Men followed the star out of the big city, along the road, into the little town of Bethlehem. They followed the star through the streets of Bethlehem, out of the nice part of town, through the not-so-nice part of town, into the

really-not-nice-at-all part of town, down a little dirt
track, until it stopped right over ... a little house.

But wait. It wasn't a palace. And there weren't any
guards. Or servants. Or flags.
Or red carpets. Or trumpets.
Or anything. Did they get it wrong?
Or was this what God meant?

Sure enough, in that little house — there, sitting on his mother's knee — they found him. The baby King.

The three men knelt before the little King. They took off their rich royal turbans and gleaming, golden crowns. They bowed their noble heads to the ground and gave him their sparkling treasures.

The journey that had begun so many centuries before had led three Wise Men here. To a little town. To a little house. To a little child.

To the King God had promised David all those years before.

But this child was a new kind of king. Though he was the Prince of Heaven, he had become poor. Though he was the Mighty God, he had become a helpless baby. This King hadn't come to be the boss. He had come to be a servant.

Heaven breaks through

The story of John the Baptist, from Matthew 3, Luke 1, 3; John 1

ABOUT THE SAME TIME Jesus was born, another baby was born. His name was John, and God had a special job for him. John was going to get everyone ready for Jesus.

The day John was born, his dad knew God's promise to Abraham was coming true — God was sending the Rescuer. And he was so happy he sang a song:

Because God loves us with a Never Stopping,
Never Giving Up, Unbreaking,
Always and Forever Love —
Heaven is breaking through!
He is sending us a Light from Heaven
To shine on us like the sun
To shine on those who live in darkness
And in the shadow of death
To guide our feet into the way of peace.

So John grew up and — well, to tell you the truth, he was a bit unusual. He lived in the desert. He wore itchy-scratchy outfits made of camel hair. He had a big, big, bushy beard and long, long, scraggly hair. And here is the oddest thing of all — he only ate locusts (short for big, creepy, crunchy, grasshoppers), which he dipped in honey (to disguise the taste, probably).

But God sent John to tell his people something important: "Stop running away from God and run to him instead," John said. "You need to be rescued. I have good news — the Rescuer is coming! Make your hearts ready for him. Yes! Get ready, because your King is coming back for you."

Great crowds listened to John. They were sorry they had sinned, and they wanted to stop running away from God. They wanted to be rescued. So John baptized them — which means he plunged them in and out of the water. It showed that they wanted to follow God and begin a new life.

One day, John was baptizing people in the Jordan River as usual when he looked up and saw a man walking down to the water's edge.

God spoke quietly to John, "This is the One!"

John's heart leapt. This was the moment he'd been waiting for all his life.

"Look," John said, as Jesus came down into the water. But his voice came out as a whisper. He couldn't make

it any louder. It was all he could do to even speak. "The Lamb of God ... God's best lamb ... who takes away the sins of the whole world."

"Will you baptize me, too?" Jesus asked.

"Who am I," John asked, "to baptize you?"

"It's what God wants me to do," Jesus said.

So John baptized Jesus.

Suddenly, it was as if someone had drawn back curtains in a dark room, as if heaven itself had opened, because a beautiful light broke through the clouds and shone down on to Jesus, bathing him in gold. Beads of water glittered and sparkled like tiny diamonds in his hair.

A white dove flew down and gently rested on Jesus.

And a voice came down from heaven. It was clear and strong and loud so everyone could hear. "This is my own Son. And I love him. I am very pleased with him," God said. "Listen to him."

Heaven had broken through.

The Great Rescue had begun…

Let's go!

Jesus is tempted in the desert and chooses his helpers,
from Matthew 4, Mark 1, Luke 4 – 6

AFTER JESUS WAS BAPTIZED, he went straight out into the desert. That might seem like an odd place to go because, as you know, deserts are very hot, and there isn't any food or water or places to stay. But Jesus needed to get away by himself and be somewhere quiet and lonely. He needed to be with his heavenly Father to get ready for his new life.

In the desert, Jesus thought about the Secret Rescue Plan he had made with God. Before the foundation of the world, they both knew what would have to happen. To rescue God's children, Jesus would have to die. There was no other way. It was the reason he had come.

Now, that old enemy — the one who had spoken through the snake to Adam and Eve, back in the garden, remember him? — he didn't want Jesus to rescue God's people. So he lied to Jesus. "Are you really God's own Son?"

he whispered. "Poor you. God must not love you. You don't need to die. Do it my way. Yes and —"

"No!" Jesus said to the liar. "I will do what God says."

And from that moment on, nothing would ever be the same.

Jesus wasn't like Adam. Jesus was a new kind of man. He would not believe the terrible lie that the enemy spoke. Jesus knew God loved him. And he would trust God. No matter what.

It was just as God had promised to Adam and Eve all those years before. Jesus had come to do battle against the snake's work. He would get rid of the sin and the darkness and the tears. And he would suffer — but he would win.

Jesus left the desert and set about the Great Rescue.
He was going to get God's people back.

But first he needed to find some helpers and friends. He
had a lot to do. He would need some people to help him.

Who would make good helpers, do you think? Clever
ones? Rich ones? Strong, important ones? Some people
might think so, but I'm sure by now you don't need me
to tell you they'd be wrong. Because the people God
uses don't have to know a lot of things, or have a lot of
things — they just have to need him a lot.

One day, Jesus was walking by the Sea of Galilee
when he saw some brothers and friends mending
their nets. They were poor fishermen.

Jesus called out to them, "Let's go!"

Peter, Andrew, James, and John looked up at this man on the shore. And they couldn't explain it: their boats needed to be put away, their nets needed mending, fish were still wriggling on the shore. But something about this stranger made them just drop their nets and their fish, leave their boats — and everything — and follow him.

This God-Man was like no one they had ever met. When they looked at Jesus, their hearts filled up with a wonderful, forever sort of happiness and inside it was as if they were running free in an open field.

Jesus asked 12 men to be his helpers: Peter, Andrew, James, and John, Matthew, Philip, Bartholomew, Thomas, another James, Simon, Thaddaeus, and Judas.

Meeting Jesus would change all of them forever.

A little girl and a poor frail lady

The story of Jairus' daughter, from Luke 8

THERE WAS ONCE a little girl who didn't get out of bed one morning, or the next, or the next. In fact, she didn't get out of bed for a whole month. She was very sick and no one knew how to make her better.

Jairus was her daddy and he loved her. One day, he was sitting by her bed, holding her hand, wishing there was something he could — "I know!" he said. He jumped to his feet, put on his coat, kissed his daughter, ran down the step, step, steps, past the servants, out of the house … through the gates, along the road, into the town, up the step, step, steps, and into the temple.

He fought his way through all the people until, at last, he found who he was looking for.

"Jesus!" he said, falling at Jesus' feet. "My daughter," he pleaded. "Please — "

But he didn't need to beg because, before he'd even finished speaking, Jesus reached out his hand and helped him up. "I'll come at once," Jesus said.

Jairus' eyes filled with tears. Jesus was coming. It would be all right.

In those days, of course, they didn't have ambulances so they had to go by foot. Jesus' helpers knew that he would heal the sick girl — but they must hurry. If Jesus didn't get there soon, it would be too late.

But everyone was in the way. Hustling and bustling. Jostling and pressing. Pushing and shoving. Squishing and squashing. The disciples ran ahead, forcing back the crowd.

Suddenly, Jesus stopped. His friends looked back. What was he doing?

"Who touched me?" Jesus asked, because he felt power go out of him.

"Me," said a frail lady looking down at the ground because she was ashamed. The poor lady had been sick for twelve years and she had to get well. She knew if she only touched Jesus' coat, she would be healed. So she touched his coat and instantly she was well.

"We don't have time!" Jesus' friends said.

But Jesus always had time. He reached out his hands and gently lifted her head. He looked into her eyes and smiled. "You believed," he said, wiping a tear from her eye, "and now you are well."

Just then, Jairus' servant rushed up to Jairus. "It's too late," he said breathlessly. "Your daughter is dead."

Jesus turned to Jairus. "It's not too late," Jesus said. "Trust me."

At Jairus' house, everyone was crying. But Jesus said, "I'm going to wake her up." Everyone laughed at him because they knew she was dead.

Jesus walked into the little girl's bedroom. And there, lying in the corner, in the shadows, was the still little figure. Jesus sat on the bed and took her pale hand.

"Honey," he said, "it's time to get up." And he reached down into death and gently brought the little girl back to life.

The little girl woke up, rubbed her eyes as if she'd just had a good night's sleep, and leapt out of bed.

Jesus threw open the shutters and sunlight flooded the dark room. "Hungry?" Jesus asked. She nodded.

Jesus called to her family, "Bring this little girl some breakfast!"

Jesus helped and healed many people, like this. He made blind people see. He made deaf people hear. He made lame people walk.

Jesus was making the sad things come untrue.

He was mending God's broken world.

How to pray

*Jesus teaches people about prayer; paraphrase of
The Lord's Prayer, from Matthew 6*

IN THOSE DAYS there were some Extra-Super-Holy People
(at least that's what they thought), and they were called
"Pharisees." Every day, they would stand out there in the
middle of the street and pray out loud in big Extra-Super-
Holy Voices. They really weren't praying so much as just
showing off. They used lots of special words that were so
clever, no one understood what they meant.

People walking by would stop and stare, which might
sound rude — except that's exactly what the Extra-Super-
Holy People wanted. They wanted everyone to say, "Look
at them. They're so holy. God must love those people best."

Now, you and I both know they were wrong —God
doesn't just love holy people. But the people walking by
weren't so sure. Perhaps you did have to be really clever, or
good, or important for God to love you. Perhaps you had
to know lots of difficult, clever words to speak to God.

So one day, Jesus taught people how to pray. He said, "When you pray, don't pray like those Extra-Super-Holy People. They think if they say lots of words, God will hear them. But it's not because you're so clever, or good, or so important, that God will listen to you. God listens to you because he loves you.

"Did you know that God is always listening to you? Did you know that God can hear the quietest whisper deep inside your heart, even before you've started to say it? Because God knows exactly what you need even before you ask him," Jesus told them.

"You see, God just can't wait to give you all that you need. So you don't need to use long words or special words. You don't have to use a special voice. You just have to talk.

"So when you pray, pray in your normal voice, just like when you're talking to someone you love very much. Like this …

Hello Daddy!
We want to know you.
And be close to you.
Please show us how.
Make everything in the world right again.
And in our hearts, too.
Do what is best — just like you do in heaven,
And please do it down here, too.
Please give us everything we need today.
Forgive us for doing wrong, for hurting you.
Forgive us just as we forgive other people
when they hurt us.
Rescue us! We need you.
We don't want to keep running away
and hiding from you.
Keep us safe from our enemies.
You're strong, God.
You can do whatever you want.
You are in charge.
Now and forever and for always!
We think you're great!
Amen!
Yes we do!

You see, Jesus was showing people that God would always love them — with a Never Stopping, Never Giving Up, Unbreaking, Always and Forever Love.

So they didn't need to hide anymore, or be afraid, or ashamed. They could stop running away from God. And they could run to him instead.

As a little child runs into her daddy's arms.

The Singer

The Sermon on the Mount, from Matthew 6, 9, and Luke 12

WHEREVER JESUS WENT, lots of people went, too. They loved being near him. Old people. Young people. All kinds of people came to see Jesus. Sick people. Well people. Happy people. Sad people. And worried people. Lots of them. Worrying about lots of things.

What if we don't have enough food? Or clothes? Or suppose we run out of money? What if there isn't enough? And everything goes wrong? And we won't be all right? What then?

When Jesus saw all the people, his heart was filled with love for them. They were like a little flock of sheep that didn't have a shepherd to take care of them. So Jesus sat them all down and he talked to them.

The people sat quietly on the grassy mountainside and listened. From where they sat, they could see the blue lake glittering below them and little fishing boats coming in from a night's catch. The spring air was fresh and clear.

"See those birds over there?" Jesus said.
Everyone looked. Little sparrows were
pecking at seeds along the stony path.

"Where do they get their food? Perhaps
they have pantries all stocked up? Cabinets
full of food?"

Everyone laughed — who's ever seen a bird
with a bag of groceries?

"No," Jesus said. "They don't need to worry
about that. Because God knows what they need
and he feeds them."

231

"And what about these wild flowers?"

Everyone looked. All around them flowers were growing. Anemones, daisies, pure white lilies.

"Where do they get their lovely clothes? Do they make them? Or do they go to work every day so they can buy them? Do they have closets full of clothes?"

Everyone laughed again — who's ever seen a flower putting on a dress?

"No," Jesus said. "They don't need to worry about that because God clothes them in royal robes of splendor! Not even a king is that well dressed!"

They had never met a king but, as they gazed out over the lake, glittering and sparkling below them, the hillsides dressed in reds, purples, and golds, they felt a great burden lift from their hearts. They could not imagine anything more beautiful.

"Little flock," Jesus said, "you are more important than birds! More important than flowers! The birds and the flowers don't sit and worry about things. And God doesn't want his children to worry either. God loves to look after the birds and the flowers. And he loves to look after you, too."

Jesus knew that God would always love and watch over the world he had made — everything in it — birds, flowers, trees, animals, everything! And, most of all, his children.

Even though people had forgotten, the birds and the flowers hadn't forgotten — they still knew their song. It was the song all of God's creation had sung to him from the very beginning. It was the song people's hearts were made to sing: "God made us. He loves us. He is very pleased with us."

It was why Jesus had come into the world: to sing them that wonderful song; to sing it not only with his voice, but with his whole life — so that God's children could remember it and join in and sing it, too.

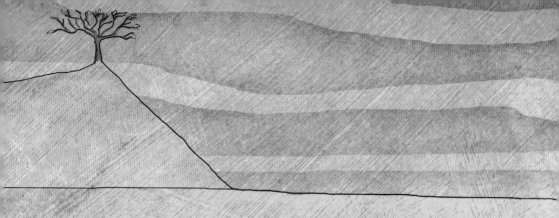

The Captain of the storm

The storm on the lake, from Mark 4 and Matthew 8

THE SUN WAS GOING DOWN. The air was warm and still.

"Let's go across the lake," Jesus said to his friends.

Jesus had been helping people all day and now he was tired. So they left the crowds at the shore and set out in a small fishing boat.

Jesus climbed into the boat to take a nap. As soon as his head touched the pillow, he fell fast asleep.

It was a beautiful evening. A gentle breeze rustled the sails. The friends were chatting happily as they headed out into the middle of the lake. Everything was perfect. Just right for a nice quiet sail …

They were only about halfway across when, out of nowhere, whirling winds swept across the lake, fierce and strong, like a hurricane! A blinding flash of lightning lit up the sky. Thunder roared right overhead!

The storm blew the water into towering waves that hurled the little boat up, up, up — then sent it hurtling, CRASHING back down, down, down!

The fishing boat was blown and buffeted and tossed and turned — back and forth and up and down and left and right and round and round!

And in the middle of the storm, Jesus was sleeping.

Now Jesus' friends had been fishermen all their lives, but in all their years fishing on this lake they had never once seen a storm like this one. No matter how hard they struggled with their ropes and sails, they couldn't control their boat. This storm was too big for them.

But the storm wasn't too big for Jesus.
"HELP!" they screamed. "Wake up! Quick, Jesus!"
Jesus opened his eyes.
"Rescue us! Save us!" they shrieked. "Don't you care?"
(Of course Jesus cared, and this was the very reason
he had come — to rescue them and to save them.)
Jesus stood up and spoke to the storm.
"Hush!" he said. That's all.
And the strangest thing happened …

The wind and the waves recognized Jesus' voice. (They had heard it before, of course — it was the same voice that made them, in the very beginning). They listened to Jesus and they did what he said.

Immediately the wind stopped. The water calmed down. It glittered innocently in the moonlight and lapped quietly against the side of the boat, as if nothing had happened.

The little boat bobbed gently up and down. There was a deep stillness and a great quiet all around.

Then Jesus turned to his wind-torn friends. "Why were you scared?" he asked. "Did you forget who I Am? Did you believe your fears, instead of me?"

Jesus' friends were quiet. As quiet as the wind and the waves. And into their hearts came a different kind of storm.

"What kind of man is this?" they asked themselves anxiously. "Even the winds and the waves obey him!" they said, because they didn't understand. They didn't realize yet that Jesus was the Son of God.

Jesus' friends had been so afraid, they had only seen the big waves. They had forgotten that, if Jesus was with them, then they had nothing to be afraid of.

No matter how small their boat — or how big the storm.

Filled full!

The Feeding of the 5,000, from Matthew 14, Mark 6, Luke 9

THERE WERE ONCE 5,000 tired and hungry (and probably very grumpy) people sitting on a hillside wanting their dinner.

They'd come to hear Jesus that day. They came before breakfast, stayed all morning, all afternoon, and way past dinner. No one had meant to be out there that long but that's how it was, listening to Jesus — as if time didn't exist. People could listen to Jesus for hours, and, on this particular day, that's just what they did.

But they hadn't brought enough food, and they couldn't just go and buy themselves a burger and fries to go because, of course, they were in the middle of nowhere with no shops or restaurants. (Besides, that kind of food wasn't invented yet.)

What would they do?

Jesus' friends had an idea. "Let's send everyone home for dinner."

"They don't need to go," Jesus said. "You can give them something to eat."

Did Jesus want them to travel all the way to town and buy food for everyone? Jesus' friends panicked. "But we don't have enough money!"

"What food do you have?" Jesus asked. "Go and see."

Now, there was a little boy in the crowd. He had brought a lunch that his mother had made for him that morning. He looked at his five loaves and two fish. It wasn't much — not nearly enough for 5,000 — but it was all he had.

"I have some," he said.

Jesus' friends laughed when they saw his little lunch. "That's not nearly enough!" they said.

But they were wrong. Jesus knew it didn't matter how much the little boy had. God would make it enough, more than enough.

Jesus said, "Bring me what you have." And so the little boy gave Jesus his lunch. Jesus winked at the little boy and whispered in his ear, "Watch!"

"How in the world will Jesus feed everyone with just that?" Jesus' friends said, because they thought it was impossible.

But Jesus knew the One who made all the fish in the oceans. And Jesus knew the One who in the very beginning had made everything out of nothing at all. How hard would something like this be for Someone like that?

Jesus took the little boy's lunch, looked up to heaven, and thanked his Father. Then Jesus gave the little lunch back to his friends.

As Jesus' friends started to hand out the food, do you know what? It was the strangest thing, no matter how much they broke off — there was always more. And more. And more. Enough for 5,000! Everyone ate as much as they wanted — second helpings, third helpings, even fourths — until they were full. And still there were leftovers.

Well, Jesus did many miracles like this. Things people thought couldn't happen, that weren't natural.

But it was the most natural thing in all the world. It's what God had been doing from the beginning, of course. Taking the nothing and making it everything. Taking the emptiness and filling it up. Taking the darkness and making it light.

Treasure hunt!

The story of the hidden treasure, from Matthew 13

ONE DAY JESUS was telling people about God's kingdom. "God's kingdom is wherever God is King," Jesus told them. "It's wherever God is in charge. It's where he fills your heart up with his Forever Happiness and you stop running away from him and you love him."

But sometimes people couldn't understand things very well. So Jesus helped them by telling them stories called "parables."

Jesus said, "God's kingdom is like a hidden treasure!" and then he told them this story …

Once upon a time, there was a man working in a field, digging. So there he is digging, but what he doesn't know is that in that field there is buried treasure. So Dig, Dig, Dig ... Klink, Klank, Klonk. UH-OH! His shovel bumps into something hard. Hello, what's this? He picks it up, dusts it off — it's a chest. It's rusted and locked but — C-R-E-E-A-K — he pries it open. What he sees inside takes his breath away: beautiful, glittering, gleaming,

twinkling, sparkling, precious jewels! It's a treasure chest!

He wants that treasure. He needs to get that treasure. He must have that treasure, somehow. Even if he has to sell everything he has so he can pay for it. He quickly buries the treasure again, runs home, and sells everything he has. He takes the money from the sale and goes and buys that field. Now he owns the field — and the treasure that is buried in it! He runs back and digs up the treasure again.

Jesus said, "Coming home to God is as wonderful as finding a treasure! You might have to dig before you find it. You might have to look before you see it. You might even have to give up everything you have to get it. But being where God is — being in his kingdom — that's more important than anything else in all the world. It's worth anything you have to give up!" Jesus told them. "Because God is the real treasure."

God had a treasure, too, of course. A treasure that was lost, long, long ago. What was God's treasure, his most important thing, the thing God loved best in all the world?

God's treasure was his children.

It was why Jesus had come into the world. To find God's treasure. And pay the price to win them back. And Jesus would do it — even if it cost him everything he had.

The Friend of little children

Jesus and the children, from Matthew 18, 19, Mark 10, Luke 18

JESUS' FRIENDS WERE ARGUING. Who was the most important helper in God's kingdom? They wanted to know.

"I am!" James said.

"No, you're not!" said Peter. "I am!"

"Nonsense," Matthew said. "I'm the cleverest!"

"No, you're not!"

"Yes, I am!"

"Yes!" "No!" "Am, too!"

This silliness went on and on like that for some time. You see, Jesus' friends had started thinking they had to do something to make themselves special to Jesus — that if they were the cleverest or the nicest or something, Jesus would like them best.

But they had forgotten something. Something God had been teaching his people all through the years: that no matter how clever you are, or how good you are, or how rich you are, or how nice you are, or how important you are — none of it makes any difference. Because God's love is a gift and, as anyone will tell you, the whole thing about a gift is, it's free. All you have to do is reach out your hands and take it.

So while Jesus' friends were arguing, some people who knew all about getting gifts — in fact, you might say they were gift-experts — had come to see Jesus. Who were they? They were little children.

Jesus' helpers tried to send them away. "Jesus doesn't have time for you!" they said. "He's too tired."

But they were wrong. Jesus always had time for children.

"Don't ever send them away!" Jesus said. "Bring the little ones to me."

Now, if you had been there, what do you think — would you have had to line up quietly to see Jesus? Do you think Jesus would have asked you how good you'd been before he'd give you a hug? Would you have had to be on your best behavior? And get dressed up? And not speak until you're spoken to?

Or … would you have done just what these children did — run straight up to Jesus and let him pick you up in his arms and swing you and kiss you and hug you and then sit you on his lap and listen to your stories and your chats?

You see, children loved Jesus, and they knew they didn't need to do anything special for Jesus to love them. All they needed to do was to run into his arms. And so that's just what they did.

Well, after all the laughing and games, Jesus turned to his helpers and said, "No matter how big you grow, never grow up so much that you lose your child's heart: full of trust in God. Be like these children. They are the most important in my kingdom."

The man who didn't have any friends (none)

The story of Zacchaeus, from Luke 19

THERE WAS ONCE A MAN who didn't have any friends (none). Do you have any friends? Well, of course you do. But not Zacchaeus. Poor Zacchaeus didn't have any.

You're probably wondering why. Was it because he was so short? (That's not a reason not to like someone.) Was it because he had a name that was hard to say? (Well, neither is that.) Even though he was short and he did have a funny name, that wasn't it. No, people didn't like Zacchaeus because he stole their money.

Zacchaeus collected taxes (taxes were what people had to pay the king), but Zacchaeus took more than he was supposed to and kept the extra money for himself and made himself rich. Everyone knew what he was up to and it made them cross and grumpy. They didn't like Zacchaeus one bit.

So they made sure he knew it by doing things like avoiding him. And walking on the opposite side of the street. And pretending not to see him. And whispering things like, "There's that nobody who thinks he's a somebody!" loud enough so he could hear.

Anyway, one day, a huge crowd gathered by the road. Jesus was coming to their town and everyone wanted to see him.

Zacchaeus wanted to see Jesus, too. But everyone was too tall. He tried jumping up and down, but that didn't work. He couldn't see a thing.

Luckily, Zacchaeus had a good idea. "I'll climb that sycamore tree!" he said. So he did. (He was surprisingly good at climbing trees for a man who was so unusually short that he had to take a flying leap just to get into his chair in the morning.)

From the tree, Zacchaeus had the perfect view — all the way down the road.

Another minute and suddenly Jesus was at the tree. He stopped and looked up. Zacchaeus saw Jesus. And Jesus saw Zacchaeus.

"Zacchaeus," Jesus said. "I'd like to come over to your house."

Zacchaeus almost fell out of the tree! Come over to his house? No one ever wanted to come anywhere near his house, let alone inside it.

The people saw this and, needless to say, it made them even crosser and grumpier than usual. They mumbled and murmured and muttered, "Why is Jesus being kind to that big sinner? Doesn't Jesus know about him?"

Zacchaeus scrambled down and took Jesus to his house. He was in a big hurry because he didn't want Jesus to change his mind. Perhaps Jesus hadn't heard about him. Perhaps Jesus didn't know about how he had been stealing. And how no one liked him. And how he didn't have any friends.

But Jesus knew — he knew all about Zacchaeus and the stealing and everything — and he still loved him.

Zacchaeus was ashamed. "Lord," he said, turning pale, "what I've done is wrong. But now I want to do the right thing. I will give the money back to everyone — four times what I stole!" And that's just what he did.

Jesus smiled. "My friend!" he said. "Today God has rescued you!"

Jesus loved Zacchaeus when nobody else did. He was Zacchaeus' friend, even when no one else was. Because Jesus was showing people what God's love was like — his wonderful, Never Stopping, Never Giving up, Unbreaking, Always and Forever Love.

Running away

The story of the lost son, from Luke 15

JESUS TOLD this story about a boy who ran away: Once upon a time, there was a boy and his dad. Now, one day, the boy gets to thinking, *Maybe if I didn't have my dad around telling me what is good for me all the time, I'd be happier. He's spoiling my fun,* he thinks. *Does my dad really want me to be happy? Does my dad really love me?* The son never thought of that before. But suddenly he doesn't know anymore.

So the son goes to his father and says, "Dad, I'm better off without you. I can look after myself. Just give me my share of your money."

His father is sad but he won't force his boy to stay. So he gives his son what he wants.

The son takes the money and goes on a long, long journey to a far off country.

And everything's wonderful and perfect — for a while. He can go wherever he wants, do whatever he wants, be whoever he wants. He is the boss, he is free!

Sometimes he gets a strange, hungry, homesick feeling inside his heart, but then he just eats more, or drinks more, or buys more clothes, or goes to more parties until it goes away.

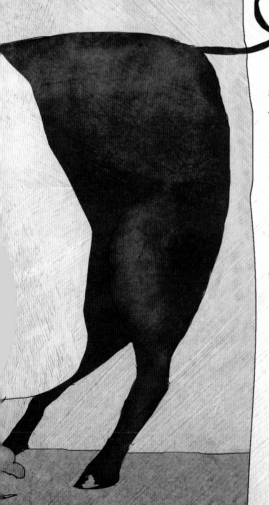

But soon his money runs out — and so do his friends. He ends up getting the only job he can find: feeding pigs. One day, he is so hungry and so desperate he even tries some piggy food —

"What am I doing?" he says suddenly, as if he has woken from a nightmare. He spits — YUCK! — all of it — ICK! — out of his mouth. "My father is rich, and here I am — in a pig sty, eating piggy food!"

He wipes his mouth and dusts himself off.

"I'm going home!"

As he starts for home though, he begins to worry. *Dad won't love me anymore. I've been too bad. He won't want me for his son anymore.* So he practices his I'm-Sorry-Speech.

All this time, what he doesn't know is that, day after day, his dad has been standing on his porch, straining his eyes, looking into the distance, waiting for his son to come home. He just can't stop loving him. He longs for the sound of his boy's voice. He can't be happy until he gets him back.

The son is still a long way off, but his dad sees him coming.

What will the dad do? Fold his arms and frown? Shout, "That'll teach you!" And, "Just you wait, young man!"

No. That's not how this story goes.

The dad leaps off the porch, races down the hill, through the gap in the hedge, up the road. Before his son can even begin his I'm-Sorry-Speech, his dad runs to him, throws his arms around him, and can't stop kissing him.

"Let's have a party!" his dad shouts. "My boy's home. He ran away. I lost him — but now I have him back!"

Jesus told them, "God is like the dad who couldn't stop loving his boy. And people are like the son who said, 'Does my dad really want me to be happy?'"

Jesus told people this story to show them what God is like. And to show people what they are like.

So they could know, however far they ran, however well they hid, however lost they were — it wouldn't matter. Because God's children could never run too far, or be too lost, for God to find them.

Washed with tears

A sinful woman anoints Jesus, from Mark 14, Luke 7, and John 12

ONE NIGHT JESUS WENT to dinner at an Important Leader's house. The Important Leader invited his Important Friends. They were all just sitting down to eat when a woman walked in. She was not invited but everyone knew who she was.

"Who does she think she is?" the guests whispered. "How dare she?" The woman was a big sinner and everyone knew it. (It was easy to see — after all, she had broken the rules and done bad things.)

The woman walked straight up to Jesus. She was carrying very expensive perfume.

Now the thing about perfume back then was that it didn't come in bottles, it came in jars. And the jars were made out of precious stone, like alabaster. But here's the catch: the jars didn't have a lid, or a stopper, or anything. So the only way you got the perfume out was if you broke the jar. Once you broke the jar, that was it — you had no more. Most people didn't use perfume because it was too precious. They just kept it on a shelf and looked at it.

So you see, this perfume was her most precious thing in all the world. It was her treasure.

The woman knelt down before Jesus like he was a king. She held Jesus' feet in her hands and started to cry. Her tears fell onto Jesus' feet, washing them. She kissed his feet and dried them with her long, dark hair. And then she did something strange. She broke the jar and poured the perfume all over his feet.

Everyone gasped. What a waste! Over someone's feet? Such expensive perfume!

It smelled like lilies in a summer field.

Jesus looked at the woman, and he smiled at her. What she had done was the most wonderful thing. Just as Samuel had anointed David, God's true king, all those years before, so this woman had anointed Jesus — not with oil, but with her tears.

The Important People were cross. They thought Jesus should not be kind to this woman. "That woman is a sinner!" they grumbled. "We're the good ones." (And it's true, they did look good — from the outside. After all, they were keeping all the rules.)

But Jesus could see inside people. And inside, in their hearts, Jesus saw that they did not love God or other people. They were running away from God, and they thought they didn't need a rescuer. They thought they were good enough because they kept the rules. But sin had stopped their hearts from working properly. And their hearts were hard and cold.

"This woman knows she's a sinner," Jesus told them. "She knows she'll never be good enough. She knows she needs me to rescue her. That's why she loves me so much.

"You look down on this woman because you don't look up to God. She is sinful on the outside — but you are sinful on the inside."

The Important People shook with anger.

Jesus turned to the woman and smiled. "Your sins are forgiven," he said. "You trusted me. And God has rescued you!"

"Who does Jesus think he is?" the Important People whispered. "Only God can forgive sins."

They didn't believe Jesus was God's Son.

The more Jesus loved people and helped them, the more the Important People and Leaders hated him. They were afraid people would follow Jesus instead of them. They were jealous. And angry… Angry enough to kill Jesus.

The Servant King

The Last Supper, from Mark 14 and John 13–14

IT WAS PASSOVER, the time when God's people remembered how God had rescued them from being slaves in Egypt. Every year they killed a lamb and ate it. "The lamb died instead of us!" they would say.

But this Passover, God was getting ready for an even Greater Rescue.

Jesus and his friends were having the Passover meal together in an upstairs room. But Jesus' friends were arguing. What about? They were arguing about stinky feet. Stinky feet? Yes, that's right. Stinky feet.

(Now the thing about feet back then was that people didn't wear shoes; they only wore sandals, which might not sound unusual, except that the streets in those days were dirty — and I don't mean just dusty dirty — I mean really stinky dirty. With all those cows and horses everywhere, you can imagine the stuff on the street that ended up on their feet!)

So anyway, someone had to wash away the dirt, but it was a dreadful job. Who on earth would ever dream of volunteering to do it?

Only the lowliest servant.

"I'm not the servant!" Peter said.

"Nor am I!" said Matthew.

Quietly, Jesus got up from the table, took off his robe, picked up a basin of water, knelt down, and started to wash his friends' feet.

"You can't," Peter said. He didn't understand about Jesus being the Servant King.

"If you don't let me wash away the dirt, Peter," Jesus said, "you can't be close to me."

Jesus knew that what people needed most was to be clean on the inside. All the dirt on their feet was nothing compared to the sin inside their hearts.

"Then wash me, Lord!" Peter said, tears filling his eyes. "All of me!"

One by one, Jesus washed everyone's feet.

"I am doing this because I love you," Jesus explained. "Do this for each other."

Now, one of Jesus'
friends had made a bad
plan. No one else knew
what the bad plan was.
But Jesus knew — and
so did Judas. Judas was
going to help the Leaders
capture Jesus — for 30
pieces of silver.

"Go on, Judas," Jesus
said. And Judas got up
from the meal, left the
room, and walked out
into the night.

Then Jesus picked up some bread and broke it. He gave it to his friends. He picked up a cup of wine and thanked God for it. He poured it out and shared it.

"My body is like this bread. It will break," Jesus told them. "This cup of wine is like my blood. It will pour out."

"But this is how God will rescue the whole world. My life will break and God's broken world will mend. My heart will tear apart — and your hearts will heal. Just as the passover lamb died, so now I will die instead of you. My blood will wash away all of your sins. And you'll be clean on the inside — in your hearts."

"So whenever you eat and drink, remember," Jesus said, "I've rescued you!"

Jesus knew it was nearly time for him to leave the world and to go back to God.

"I won't be with you long," he said. "You are going to be very sad. But God's Helper will come. And then you'll be filled up with a Forever Happiness that won't ever leave. So don't be afraid. You are my friends and I love you."

Then they sang their favorite song. And walked up to their favorite place, an olive garden.

A dark night in the garden

The Garden of Gethsemane, from Luke 22, Mark 14, John 18

THE WIND WAS picking up now, blowing clouds across the moon, shrouding the garden in darkness.

"Stay up with me?" Jesus asked his friends. They said yes and waited under the olive trees, but they were tired and soon they fell asleep.

Jesus walked ahead alone, into the dark. He needed to talk to his heavenly Father.

He knew it was time for him to die. They had planned it long ago, he and his Father. Jesus was going to take the punishment for all the wrong things anybody had ever done, or ever would do.

"Papa! Father!" Jesus cried. And he fell to the ground. "Is there any other way to get your children back? To heal their hearts? To get rid of the poison?"

But Jesus knew — there was no other way. All the poison of sin was going to have to go into his own heart.

God was going to pour into Jesus' heart all the sadness and brokenness in people's hearts. He was going to pour into Jesus' body all the sickness in people's bodies. God was going to have to blame his son for everything that had gone wrong. It would crush Jesus.

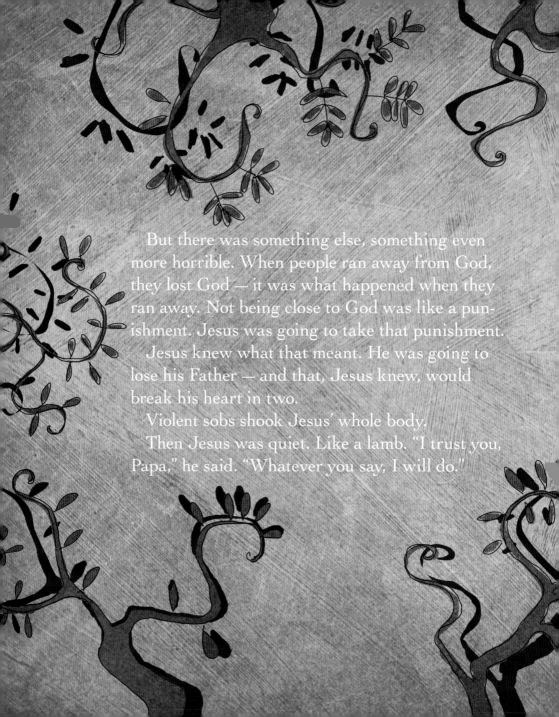

But there was something else, something even more horrible. When people ran away from God, they lost God — it was what happened when they ran away. Not being close to God was like a punishment. Jesus was going to take that punishment.

Jesus knew what that meant. He was going to lose his Father — and that, Jesus knew, would break his heart in two.

Violent sobs shook Jesus' whole body.

Then Jesus was quiet. Like a lamb. "I trust you, Papa," he said. "Whatever you say, I will do."

Suddenly, through the trees, a glitter of starlight flashed off steel. Into the quiet garden came whispers, muffled voices, clanking metal — and the sound of boots marching.

Jesus stood up.

He woke his friends. "Now is the time," he said gently. "Everything that was written about me — what God has been telling his people all through the long years — it's all coming true."

And into the night, with burning torches and lanterns, with swords and clubs and armor, they came — an army of soldiers. Judas led them straight to Jesus so they could arrest him.

Jesus was waiting for them.

Peter leapt up, took a sword, and tried to defend Jesus. He sliced off a guard's ear. Jesus immediately touched the guard and healed him.

"Peter," he said, "this is not the way."

Peter didn't realize that no army, no matter how big, could ever arrest Jesus. Not unless Jesus let them.

Then Jesus, who had never done anything except love people, was arrested, as if he were a criminal.

Jesus' friends were afraid. So they ran away and hid in the dark shadows.

The guards marched Jesus off and took him to the Leaders.

The Leaders put Jesus on trial. "Are you the Son of God?" they asked.

"I Am," Jesus said.

"Who do you think you are? To call yourself God? You must die for calling yourself the Son of God!"

Only the Romans were allowed to kill prisoners, so the Leaders made a plan. "We'll tell the Romans, 'This man wants to be our king!' And then they will crucify him."

But it would be all right. It was God's Plan.

"It was for this reason that I was born into the world," Jesus said.

The sun stops shining

The Crucifixion, from Matthew 27, Mark 15, Luke 23, John 19

"SO YOU'RE A KING, are you?" the Roman soldiers jeered. "Then you'll need a crown and a robe."

They gave Jesus a crown made out of thorns. And put a purple robe on him. And pretended to bow down to him. "Your Majesty!" they said.

Then they whipped him. And spat on him. They didn't understand that this was the Prince of Life, the King of heaven and earth, who had come to rescue them.

The soldiers made him a
sign — "Our King" and nailed it
to a wooden cross.
They walked up a hill outside the
city. Jesus carried the cross on his
back. Jesus had never done anything
wrong. But they were going to kill him
the way criminals were killed.

They nailed Jesus to the cross.

"Father, forgive them," Jesus gasped. "They don't understand what they're doing."

"You say you've come to rescue us!" people shouted. "But you can't even rescue yourself!"

But they were wrong. Jesus could have rescued himself. A legion of angels would have flown to his side — if he'd called.

"If you were really the Son of God, you could just climb down off that cross!" they said.

And of course they were right. Jesus could have just climbed down. Actually, he could have just said a word and made it all stop. Like when he healed that little girl. And stilled the storm. And fed 5,000 people.

But Jesus stayed.

You see, they didn't understand. It wasn't the nails that kept Jesus there. It was love.

"Papa?" Jesus cried, frantically searching the sky. "Papa? Where are you? Don't leave me!"

And for the first time — and the last — when he spoke, nothing happened. Just a horrible, endless silence. God didn't answer. He turned away from his Boy.

Tears rolled down Jesus' face. The face of the One who would wipe away every tear from every eye.

Even though it was midday, a dreadful darkness covered the face of the world. The sun could not shine. The earth trembled and quaked. The great mountains shook. Rocks split in two. Until it seemed that the whole world would break. That creation itself would tear apart.

The full force of the storm of God's fierce anger at sin was coming down. On his own Son. Instead of his people. It was the only way God could destroy sin, and not destroy his children whose hearts were filled with sin.

Then Jesus shouted out in a loud voice, "It is finished!"

And it was. He had done it. Jesus had rescued the whole world.

"Father!" Jesus cried. "I give you my life." And with a great sigh he let himself die.

Strange clouds and shadows filled the sky. Purple, orange, black. Like a bruise.

Jesus' friends gently carried Jesus. They laid Jesus in a new tomb carved out of rock.

How could Jesus die? What had gone wrong? What did it mean? They didn't know anything anymore. Except they did know their hearts were breaking.

"That's the end of Jesus," the Leaders said.

But, just to be sure, they sent strong soldiers to guard the tomb. They hauled a huge stone in front of the door to the tomb. So that no one could get in.

Or out.

God's wonderful surprise

The Resurrection, from Matthew 28, Mark 16, Luke 24, John 20

JESUS' FRIENDS WERE SAD. They would never see their best friend again. How could this happen? Wasn't Jesus the Rescuer? The King God had promised? It wasn't supposed to end like this.

Yes, but whoever said anything about the end?

Just before sunrise, on the third day, God sent an earthquake — and an angel from heaven. When the guards saw the angel, they fell down with fright. The angel rolled the huge stone away, sat on top of it, and waited.

At the first glimmer of dawn, Mary Magdalene and other women headed to the tomb to wash Jesus' body. The early morning sun slanted through the ancient olive trees, drops of dew glittering on leaves and grasses — little tears everywhere. The friends walked quietly along the hilly path, through the olive groves, until they reached the tomb. And immediately noticed something odd — it was wide open.

They peered through the opening into the dark tomb. But wait. Jesus' body was gone!

And something else: a shining man was there, with clothes made from lightning.

"Don't be scared," the angel said.

But (they couldn't help it) they screamed anyway.

The angel asked them, "What are you doing here? This is a tomb and tombs are for dead people."

The women couldn't speak.

"Jesus isn't dead anymore!" he said. "He's alive again!"

And their hearts leapt. And then the angel laughed with such gladness that they felt, for a moment, as if they had woken from a nightmare.

The other women rushed home, but Mary stayed
behind. How could it be true? Jesus was definitely
dead — how could he be alive? Just then Mary heard
someone else in the garden. *Perhaps it's the gardener,* she
thought. *He'll know where Jesus' body is.*

"I don't know where Jesus is!" Mary said urgently.
"I can't find him."

But it was all right. Jesus knew where she was. And he
had found her.

"Mary!"

Only one person said her name like that. She could
hear her heart thumping. She turned around. She could
just make out a figure. She shaded her eyes to see ...
and thought she was dreaming.

But she wasn't dreaming. She was seeing.

"Jesus!"

Mary fell to the ground. Sudden tears filled her eyes
and great sobs shook her whole body, and all she wanted
in that moment was to cling to Jesus and never let him go.

"You'll be able to hold on to me later, Mary," Jesus said
gently, "and always be close to me. But now, go and tell
the others that I'm alive!"

Mary ran and ran, all the way to the city. She had
never run so fast or so far in all her life. She felt she
could have run forever. She didn't even feel like her feet
touched the ground. The sun seemed to be dancing and
gleaming and bounding across the sky, racing with her
and shining brighter than she could ever remember in
the clear, fresh air.

And it seemed to her that morning, as she ran, almost
as if the whole world had been made anew, almost as if
the whole world was singing for joy — the trees,
tiny sounds in the grass, the birds … her heart.

Was God really making everything sad come
untrue? Was he making even death come untrue?
    She couldn't wait to tell Jesus' friends. "They
won't believe it!" she laughed.
    She was right, of course.

Going home

The Ascension, from Matthew 28, Mark 16, Luke 24, John 14

JESUS' FRIENDS WERE AFRAID. So they were hiding in an upstairs room with the door bolted shut.

But that didn't stop Jesus. He just walked straight through the wall.

"It's a ghost!" Thomas screamed and hid under the table.

But it wasn't a ghost.

"I'm hungry," Jesus said. "What's for lunch?"

Peter gave him a fish. They all hung back and watched him eat it. *This can't be,* they were telling themselves. *It's impossible. It's not happening.*

But it was — right in front of them.

"Delicious!" Jesus wiped his mouth with the back of his hand and grinned. "Can a ghost do that?" He winked. And then they all laughed.

"I'm really here!" Jesus said.

And he really was.

Peter's heart leaped with joy and he fell into Jesus' arms, hugging and kissing him. The others followed. They felt their hearts would burst from the happiness.

The friends ate together and chatted happily. And every now and then, they'd just gaze at Jesus, and have to touch him to be sure they weren't dreaming.

Jesus had a real body but this body was better. It had come through death and couldn't get sick or be killed again. This body would live forever. Jesus had come back with a brand new body.

Not only were sad things coming untrue, the friends realized, they were becoming new again. Was God going to make everything new?

Jesus said, "I am the Savior and the Rescuer of the world." And they knew, because he couldn't stay dead, because Jesus had come alive again, that somehow everything would be all right.

A few days later, as they walked together, Jesus told his friends, "It's time for me to go home to my Father."

They all looked worried. And then they remembered what Jesus had told them before he died. "There's a place for you. I'll get it ready," Jesus had said. "You know the way."

Thomas had panicked. "I don't know the way to get there!"

"Yes, you do," Jesus had said. "I am the Way and the Truth and the Life."

When at last they reached the top of the highest hill near Jerusalem, Jesus turned to them and said, "Go everywhere and tell everyone the happy news!"

"Tell them I love them so much that I died for them. It's the Truth that overcomes the terrible lie. God loves his children. Yes, he really does!"

Suddenly the whole sky was filled with a dazzling light.

"Now everyone can come home to God," Jesus said. "Death is not the end of you. You can live forever with your Father in heaven because I have rescued the whole world!"

And something amazing happened: Jesus rose up into the bright air, higher and higher. They shaded their eyes and watched him go, until a cloud hid Jesus so they couldn't see him anymore. They stood looking up into the sky like that for a long time.

Suddenly two shining men appeared. "What are you doing?" they asked. "Jesus has gone up to heaven. But one day he will come back. In the same way you saw him leave. From heaven. And from the sky."

Jesus' friends went back to Jerusalem with a strange gladness inside their hearts. And something Jesus said that stuck in their minds: "Even though you won't be able to see me anymore, I will never leave you. No! Not ever! I will be with you. Yes! Always and forever!"

"How can Jesus be with us and leave us at the same time?" they wondered.

They didn't understand.

No, but soon they would.

God sends help

Pentecost, from Acts 1 – 5; John 15

JESUS' FRIENDS AND HELPERS huddled together in a
stuffy upstairs room. Even though it was sunny outside,
the shutters were closed. The door was locked.

"Wait in Jerusalem," Jesus had told them, "I am going
to send you a special present. God's power is going to
come into you. God's Holy Spirit is coming."

So here they were. Waiting. Actually, mostly
what they were doing was just being scared and hiding.
(You can't blame them – their best friend had left; the
Important People and Leaders were after them; and
Jesus had given them a job they didn't know how to do.)

As they waited, they were praying and remembering —
remembering how, from the beginning, God had been
working out his Secret Rescue Plan.

Suddenly, a strong wind filled the little room, whistling through the walls, rustling the straw on the floor. And there — on everyone's heads, shining in the gloom — were flickering flames. Fire that didn't hurt or burn.

And something more: inside, in their hearts, they felt a strange heat, almost as if all the coldness and hardness were melting away. As if their broken hearts were mending. And God was giving them brand new hearts — hearts that could work properly.

How it happened they didn't know, but they knew God's power had struck their hearts ablaze — and Jesus himself was coming to live inside them.

They had seen Jesus go away, but now he was closer than he had ever been — inside their hearts. And this time nothing could ever separate them. Jesus would always be there. With them. Loving them. Whispering the promise that would get rid of the poison and the terrible lie and the sickness in their hearts. God's wonderful promise to them: "You are my child. And I love you."

"Make your home in me, as I make my home in you," Jesus had said.

Could it be? Heaven was coming into their hearts.

They threw open the shutters. Sunlight flooded their room, as love had flooded their hearts. And the little room was filled with happy noises. Dancing feet, singing, laughing.

They unlocked the door and surged out into the streets — as if they had never been afraid.

Peter spoke in a loud voice, so everyone could hear: "Jesus died for you!" he said. "Because he loves you. But God made him alive again. He has rescued you!"

People stopped. And listened. The words sank down deep into their hearts and worked like a medicine that makes you well. Like the antidote to a deadly poison. Like a kiss that wakes you from a deep sleep.

"Stop running away from God!" Peter said. "Run to him instead! So he can love you. And make you free!"

And Peter told them the wonderful Story of God's Love — God's Never Stopping, Never Giving Up, Unbreaking, Always and Forever Love. How Jesus had come. All that had happened.

There were lots of people from faraway countries in Jerusalem. They couldn't speak the same language but as they listened to Peter, everyone could understand what he was saying — in their own languages!

Many people believed. And became Jesus' new friends and helpers. And the wonderful news of Jesus spread. Like sparks from a fire. To villages. Towns. Cities.

Every day, more and more people believed.

And so it was that the family of God's children, his special people, grew.

One man was watching. "I'll stop this!" Saul said.

But this was God's Plan. And nothing in all the world would ever be able to stop it.

A new way to see

The story of Paul, from Acts 6 – 9, 12 – 28;
Colossians 2, Romans 8, Ephesians 2

OF ALL THE PEOPLE who kept the rules, Saul was the best.

"I'm good at being good!" he'd tell you.

He was very proud. And very good. But he wasn't very nice.

Saul hated anyone who loved Jesus. He traveled around looking for them. He wanted to catch them and put them in prison. He wanted everyone to forget all about Jesus. He didn't believe Jesus was the Rescuer. And he didn't believe Jesus was alive, either.

You see, Saul had never met Jesus.

So one day, Jesus met Saul.

SAUL

Saul was on his way to Damascus when suddenly a dazzling light flashed like lightning. It was brighter than the sun. It was too bright. Saul shielded his eyes and fell to the ground.

He heard a loud voice. It was too loud. It gave Saul a headache.

"Saul! Saul!" said the loud voice. "Why are you fighting me?"

"Lord?" Saul answered, "Who are you?"

"I am Jesus," said the voice. "When you hurt my friends, you are hurting me, too." Saul's whole body trembled.

"Go to the city," Jesus said. "I'll tell you what to do."

When Saul opened his eyes, he couldn't see. His helpers had to hold his hand and lead him like a little child. Saul was blind for three whole days — and yet it was as if he was seeing for the very first time.

Meanwhile, there was a man called Ananias who loved Jesus. Jesus came to him in a dream: "Go to Saul and pray for him, and I will make him see again."

Ananias knew all about Saul and how he hated Jesus' followers. "Lord, he has come to hurt us!"

But Jesus told Ananias, "Saul is the one I've chosen to tell the whole world who I am."

So Ananias went to Saul. "Brother Saul," Ananias said, "it was Jesus you met on the road." And Ananias prayed for Saul.

Suddenly Saul could see again, but he saw everything differently. He wasn't mean anymore. He even changed his name from Saul to Paul, which means "small" and "humble" — the very opposite of proud.

And do you know what Ananias' name means? "The Lord is full of Grace." (Grace is just another word for gift — which is funny, because that's just what Paul's message was all about from then on.)

PAUL

"It's not about keeping rules!" Paul told people. "You don't have to be good at being good for God to love you. You just have to believe what Jesus has done and follow him. Because it's not about trying, it's about trusting. It's not about rules, it's about Grace: God's free gift — that cost him everything."

What had happened to Paul? He met Jesus.

Paul got a new job. He called himself a servant and traveled everywhere telling everyone about Jesus. He got shipwrecked — three times! He even ended up in prison.

"God loves us!" he wrote from prison. "Nothing can ever — no, not ever! — separate us from the Never Stopping, Never Giving Up, Unbreaking, Always and Forever Love of God he showed us in Jesus!"

And so it was, just as God promised Abraham that dark night all those years before, the family of God's children grew and grew.

Until one day, they would come to number more than even all the stars in the sky.

A dream of heaven

John sees into the future, from Revelation 1, 5, 21, 22

JOHN WAS ONE OF Jesus' helpers. He was old now and living on an island, which might sound nice except it was a prison. (The Leaders put him there to stop him from talking about Jesus, but I'm sure you don't think a little thing like being in a cell, in a prison, on an island, in the middle of an ocean, could stop God's Plan, do you?)

One morning, Jesus appeared — right there, in John's cell. Jesus' eyes were bright, shining like the sun. "I am going to show you a secret, John," Jesus said, "about when I come back." His voice was like the sound of rushing waters. "Write down what you see so God's children can read it, and wait with happy excitement."

Then Jesus gave John a beautiful dream — except John was wide awake and what he saw was real and one day it would all come true...

I see a throne. And on the throne is a king.
And the King is Jesus. All around the throne
people are bowing down. They are giving him
their treasures.

There are loud cheers and
clapping, clapping and bright
laughter like a thousand waterfalls
and everyone bursts out singing
a new song...

"This is our King! The Lamb who died, so we don't have to – our Rescuer. All Honor and Glory! Forever and ever." And every creature everywhere, in heaven and on earth and under the earth and in the sea, joins in.

And then

From all around

A wide

Immense

Beautiful

S i l e n c e

And I see Satan – God's horrible enemy – thrown down, defeated.

I see a sparkling city shimmering in the sky;
glittering, glowing – coming down!
From heaven.
And from the sky.
Heaven is coming down to earth!

God's city is beautiful. Walls of topaz, jasper, sapphire. Wide streets
paved with gold. Gleaming pearl gates that are never locked shut.

Where is the sun? Where is the moon?
They aren't needed anymore. God is all the
Light people need! No more darkness!
No more night!

And the King says, "Look! God and his children are together again. No more running away. Or hiding. No more crying or being lonely or afraid. No more being sick or dying.

Because all those things are gone.

Yes, they're gone forever.

Everything sad has come untrue.

And see – I have wiped away every tear from every eye!"

And then a deep, beautiful voice that sounded like thunder in the sky says, "Look, I am making everything new!"

It was hard to squeeze all John saw into words. And fit it onto a page. And cram it into a book. All the words on all the pages of all the books in all the world would never be enough.

"I am the Beginning," Jesus said, "and the Ending!"

One day, John knew, Heaven would come down and mend God's broken world and make it our true, perfect home once again.

And he knew, in some mysterious way that would be hard to explain, that everything was going to be more wonderful for once having been so sad.

And he knew then that the ending of The Story was going to be so great, it would make all the sadness and tears and everything seem like just a shadow that is chased away by the morning sun.

"I'm on my way," said Jesus. "I'll be there soon!"

John came to the end of his book. But he didn't write "The End." Because, of course, that's how stories finish. (And this one's not over yet.)

So instead, he wrote: "Come quickly, Jesus!"

Which, perhaps, is really just another way of saying ...

To be
continued...

Paraphrase of John 1:12 – 13

For anyone who says yes to Jesus
For anyone who believes what Jesus said
For anyone who will just reach out to take it
Then God will give them this wonderful gift:

To be born into
A whole new Life
To be who they really are
Who God always made them to be —
Their own true selves —
God's dear
Child.

Because, you see, the most wonderful thing
about this Story is — it's your story, too!

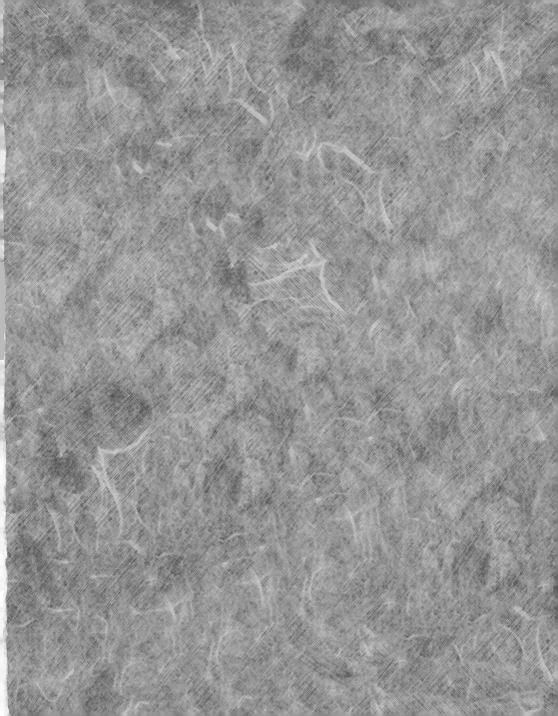

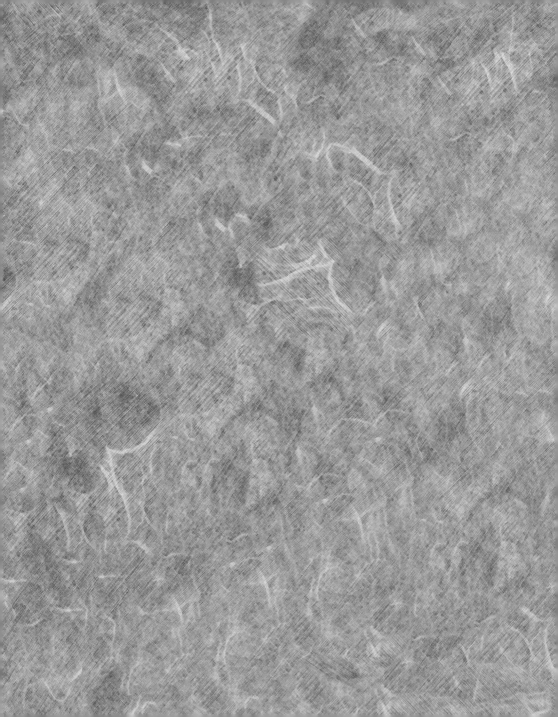